TRUE LEADERS INSPIRE FOLLOWERS

(...TO BE BETTER LEADERS THAN THEMSELVES)

This book is a compilation of some of my ideas and life experiences, along with ideas, sayings, and writings that I have borrowed from Albert Einstein, Sir Isaac Newton, Jesus, Mahatma Gandhi, and others. If you don't like their words, whose would you choose?

Author: Newton Benjamin Fernandez

"A job title, like a tattoo is merely an imprint, but one's character is a footprint: daily evidence of your own choices along life's journey."

Published by Hemingway Publishers

Cover design by Hemingway Publishers

ISBN: Printed in the United States

HEMINGWAY
PUBLISHERS

Table of Contents

Acknowledgments

I would like to express my deepest gratitude to the crucible of life—my family. Hence, I dedicate this book to Sandra, my faithful wife and companion who has stuck with me through thick and thin, and to my beloved children and cherished grandchildren. Their unwavering support, endless inspiration, and boundless joy have filled my life with meaning and purpose. I began writing this book approximately 10 years ago. Then, for a while, I had to slow down and put my writing on the back burner, trusting our good Lord to slowly but surely help me row to shore. Their love and belief in me have kept me going, even during the toughest moments.

I am also immensely grateful to the team at Hemingway Publishers for their invaluable feedback and guidance. Their keen insights and attention to detail have helped shape this book into its final form. Special thanks to my friends at the Divine Mercy prayer group, especially Violette Doummar, and Fr. Anish Alex at St. Joseph Parish, Mississauga, Ontario. who have provided encouragement, advice, and moral support along the way. Your encouragement has meant the world to me.

I want to thank an old friend, Michael Bunyan, whom the Lord used to draw me to HIM. Finally, my sincere thanks go to the readers who will embark on this journey with me. Your interest in my work is the greatest reward an author could ask for. Thank you all for being part of this incredible journey. May our Lord move in the lives of all leaders, not just in our secular world but also in various other positions. May this be a constant reminder to us that a good leader is a good leader everywhere.

Prologue

"It is a terrible thing to look over your shoulder when you are trying to lead — and find no one there."[1]

Franklin D Roosevelt

In the absence of a leadership role model, I have witnessed several colleagues who appear fearless in supervisory positions suddenly deteriorate and indulge in fear-based practices. There are times when I have wondered why a mindset exists in the workplace that managing requires you to "know it all," look and behave intimidatingly, and wield power because you hold the title.

"Become the kind of leader that people would follow voluntarily, even if you had no title or position."[2]

Brian Tracy

Job titles reflect your job description—nothing more, nothing less. Titles may provide you with a semblance of authority, but they cannot automatically provide you with the qualities you need to be effective in the workplace daily. Over the past several years in Canada and the USA, I encountered managers in my office almost every day wanting to "write someone up" or bring the hammer down on an employee. I agree that disciplinary steps are sometimes needed to raise awareness, and to alert an employee who is failing to meet expectations. However, before one reaches that point, it is important for leaders and managers to be unbiased. It is better to first raise the matter with the employee informally, opening a dialogue based on respect and understanding. Collaborative problem-solving offers several benefits, and at the same time, it sets the tone for other employees to recognize that a leader is approachable and genuinely caring.

If given a choice, most people would prefer to be a "leader" rather than a "follower," especially the ambitious among us. The term "follower" has often been saddled with negative connotations because it implies a lack of independence or originality. It suggests someone who simply follows the lead of others rather than thinking for themselves or taking initiative. However, followers can also play important roles in various contexts, such as supporting leaders, contributing ideas, and executing tasks effectively.

Stephen R. Covey, in his book, states that "Management is efficiency in climbing the ladder of success; leadership determines whether the ladder is leaning against the right wall."[3] - However, I cannot help but note that as you climb this ladder, you need to stop and strengthen each rung you leave behind, so others can safely follow.

In making this statement about managers and leaders, I do not wish to separate the skills required to lead from the ability to manage. In fact, I see both of them as two sides of the same coin. On one hand, managing a business requires a knowledgeable person who is responsible for establishing, communicating, training, and enforcing rules, accurately designed policies, and procedures to attain productivity and profitability. While an organization can possess the most elaborate management systems, ultra-modern "plug & play" computerized training programs, various machinery, and tools in place, it will never be able to "hit the ground running" and accomplish its goals without an organization's biggest asset – It's people.

When I discussed these thoughts with a colleague, his response was quick: "Just hire the right people, and your problems will be solved." I presumed this was a tongue-in-cheek comment. However, unlike rules and policies, the people you work with have desires and aspirations; some are ambitious, while others are simply looking for a way to achieve a means to an end. Some may choose to follow, while others might just pretend to follow when the boss is watching. People are free to choose whether to obey or not. The obvious word is choice – in this word lies the key to unlocking the potential that rests in our hearts. Reactive thinking occurs when a stimulus gives rise to an immediate response, while proactivity occurs when there is sufficient space between the stimulus and the response for a choice to be made. "Attitude is a choice. Happiness is a choice. Optimism is a choice. Kindness is a choice. Giving is a choice. Respect is a choice. Whatever choice you make makes you. Choose wisely."[4] It is impossible not to notice that all our leadership choices concern people.

My goal in writing this book is to help leaders and inspire followers to become better leaders than themselves.

Chapter 1

Who Can Teach & Whom Can I Follow?

During the COVID-19 pandemic, many of us could not help but wonder about the future, the discovery of a vaccine, the recurrence of the virus, and a myriad of similar questions that plague our society. Fear grips us when we think about the toll this has taken on lives that have changed forever. As individuals and families, we are concerned about the economy, the job losses, and the financial impact this will have on us. Fear is not the opposite of faith but the absence of it. In fact, I am convinced that the opposite of fear is belief. The question stood out like a sign on a billboard: In whom shall I trust? In whom shall I believe? Whom can I follow?

A few decades ago, my own search for a trusting example of leadership was a struggle. It is disappointing to realize that just when you have selected your role model, he soon admits failure and changes direction. You soon realize that the help of men and women is in vain because people change, plans change, ideas change, minds change, and even goals are altered.

Dan Schawbel, in h is blog at quickbase.com, lists10 reasons why leaders fail:

"1. Leaders become selfish. 2. They stop navigating the team. 3. Leaders become greedy. 4. They get arrogant. 5. They focus too much on politics. 6. They don't give enough criticism. 7. Leaders refuse to adapt. 8. They don't understand self-discipline. 9. They are too reactive. 10. Leaders do not communicate well."[5]

I have deduced that these ten behaviors stem from three basic human frailties and, if not harnessed and redirected, can cause the leader to fail. In the following chapters, we will explore examples of three such significant leaders in antiquity and how three human weaknesses caused them to fail even though they had everything they needed to be successful.

1. **The untamed and unbridled ego of a chosen person.**

2. **The licentious power of a privileged person.**

3. **The unteachable spirit of a person in need of self-discipline.**

The untamed and unbridled ego of a chosen person:

Managers and leaders are hired because of their skills, knowledge, and experience. However, over time, due to their selfish ego and pride, the team's operational needs are overshadowed by their personal greed. A good leader leads the team from the bottom up and not from the top down. A good leader is there to serve his team daily and help each member succeed individually to meet the goals of the organization. When the team succeeds, the leader succeeds, and in turn, the corporation begins to see the good times roll. The signs of leadership going wrong are when you see a leader becoming power-hungry and seeking control rather than giving advice, feeling threatened by meaningful questions instead of keeping an open mind to see opportunities for growth, and adopting a dictatorial stance instead of a nurturing mentoring attitude which automatically sends out a message that you care.

Leaders who hire well, train, and value their employees are those who can delegate tasks and ensure that everyone on their team is learning, growing, and being challenged. When leaders do not send out a clear message to their team that they care about everyone as decent and trustworthy human beings within the organization, it begins to erode trust, and work suffers. This forces the leader to start micromanaging his team to the detriment of the employer-employee working relationship. This results in a lack of employee engagement due to a lack of transparency. Leaders who micromanage can end up hurting themselves. They become stressed out because they are overloaded with work, and their employees feel disillusioned and undervalued, and this negatively affects employee retention. One can easily recognize an egotistical micromanager by his communication style, which often favors the pronoun "I" instead of "we."

My research in historical antiquity felt important for several reasons:

Our immediate instinct draws us to understand the present advancement of knowledge, insights, and lessons from cultural diversity. Also, the latest innovations are driven by present successful people and Leadership styles. However, human development has happened over time, and just like the present times we live in, decades from now we will also encounter successful people. This does not mean that decades from now, we will look back with disdain.

We have witnessed great strides from the Paleolithic to the Bronze Age to the Iron Age to the Industrial Age, and from then on, we progressed in leaps and bounds to digital and information technology while exploring the study and application of Artificial Intelligence for the benefit of humankind. However, the heart of humankind has remained the same, swinging like a pendulum from insecurity to pride, misunderstanding his pride to be his strength.

Bolstering in our minds our own self-reliant prowess. This prompts me to realize that there ought to be nuggets of wisdom in every phase of human development, and it is up to us to recognize and learn from ancient history and gain insights into how human societies developed over time.

Just as we would prefer future generations to look back and appreciate the successes of our times, we, too, must take time to study ancient history and learn how human societies have evolved. This can provide a tangible connection to our past and can foster a sense of identity and continuity. Historical antiquity can offer valuable lessons. By studying the successes and failures of ancient civilizations, we can learn about human behavior, governance, economics, and environmental management, which can inform contemporary decision-making.

Research in antiquity can invariably provide us with interdisciplinary insights not just into archaeology, anthropology, history, and art history but also into Leadership styles, their successes and failures. It can contribute to the overall advancement of knowledge, where each discovery or new interpretation adds to the collective understanding of human history and refines existing theories. This, I believe, is a step forward along the journey of humankind to build a better future.

Historical Leadership perspective in Antiquity: History gives us great insight into the life of King Solomon. My research amazed me by revealing how little has changed in the 21st-century styles of leadership in comparison. There are many lessons to be learned from Solomon's life and his wisdom. King Solomon's life contains many lessons and mistakes he made that we need to avoid as Christians today. Dubbed the wisest human who has ever lived, King Solomon has valuable life lessons he can teach us that are outlined in the book of Proverbs, one of the books of the Bible. Proverbs are a collection of wise sayings and teachings, mostly attributed to King Solomon, known for his practical wisdom on various aspects of life.

As described in various biblical manuscripts such as 1 Kings and 2 Chronicles, despite being the wisest man and king who had great wisdom from the Lord, King Solomon made some mistakes in his life that we need to avoid today both as leaders at home and as well as in the workplace. King Solomon, renowned for his wisdom and wealth, also had significant faults that contributed to his downfall:

1. Idolatry: Despite his wisdom, Solomon fell into idolatry by allowing his foreign wives to influence him to worship their gods. This departure from worshiping Yahweh led to divine punishment.

2. Extravagance and Oppression: Solomon's opulent building projects, including the construction of the temple and his own palace, required heavy taxation and forced labor, leading to oppression and resentment among the people.

3. Multiple Marriages: Solomon had numerous wives, many of whom were foreign princesses he married for political alliances. These marriages violated God's command against intermarriage with pagan nations and ultimately led to his spiritual downfall.

4. Failure to Follow God's Laws: Despite his initial wisdom and devotion to God, Solomon gradually drifted away from God's commandments, leading to moral compromise and spiritual decline.

5. Succession Issues: Solomon's failure to establish a clear succession plan resulted in turmoil and division after his death, with the kingdom eventually splitting into two separate entities.

Overall, Solomon's downfall stemmed from a combination of moral compromise, idolatry, oppression, and failure to uphold God's commandments despite his initial wisdom and devotion. Solomon's fall can be attributed to his inability to control his ego.

The licentious power of a privileged person:

When Leaders are satisfied with the positive state of the company and their team, they must not forget the principles that made them successful in the first place. They must continue to direct people forward, maintaining clear visions and goals to make sure that everyone is constantly delivering high-quality results and that the overall company is benefiting. Leaders must set expectations not only for their team but also for themselves, keep track of everyone's progress, and remain accountable.

Even the best may think they know everything, which can lead to their downfall. Leaders need to be continuous learners if they want to keep up with the challenging demands of today's economy. The employees and the people you meet outside the office can really help you make better decisions; you should listen to them. If you ignore what other people say, it's going to make your job harder because people may oppose it, and you might be left stranded.

Leaders must refrain from playing politics and trying to manipulate people for their own selfish purposes. A good leader must show courage in the face of challenges and take responsibility for all outcomes. Courage is not the opposite of fear, but it is the ability to do the right thing in the face of fear.

It's very easy for leaders to try and please everyone and to befriend coworkers but that's not always effective. You must take a step back, look at the weaknesses of your team, and discuss with them how they can improve. If all you do is compliment everyone, then you are doing them a disservice. At the same time, you should accept criticism from them. Some of your leadership tactics might not be best for the group, and you need to know that.

Historical Perspective in Antiquity: Rehoboam was indeed the son of Solomon and, thus, the heir to the throne. However, his succession to kingship wasn't automatic. After Solomon's death, a dispute arose over the succession. Rehoboam faced opposition, particularly from Jeroboam, which led to the division of the Kingdom of Israel into two separate entities: the Northern Kingdom of Israel and the Southern Kingdom of Judah, with Rehoboam ruling over Judah. Given the privilege of becoming King, he also made several critical mistakes that led to his downfall:

1. Arrogance and Harshness: When faced with the people's request for relief from Solomon's oppressive policies, Rehoboam rejected the advice of the elders to be gentle and instead listened to the counsel of his younger peers, responding with harshness and arrogance. He famously declared, "My little finger is thicker than my father's loins"[6] (1 Kings 12:10), indicating his intent to rule with even greater severity than his father.

2. Failure to Listen to Counsel: Rehoboam's refusal to heed the elders' wisdom and his reliance on the advice of his inexperienced friends alienated many of his subjects, leading to rebellion and the eventual division of the kingdom.

3. Loss of Support: Rehoboam's oppressive policies and heavy-handed rule caused widespread discontent among the people, resulting in ten of the twelve tribes breaking away to form the Northern Kingdom of Israel under the leadership of Jeroboam.

4. Inability to Reconcile: Even after the northern tribes' rebellion, Rehoboam attempted to regain control through military force rather than seeking reconciliation or compromise, further entrenching the division and weakening his own position.

5. Weak Leadership: Rehoboam's inability to effectively govern and unite the kingdom led to continued instability and conflict throughout his reign, ultimately resulting in the decline of the Southern Kingdom of Judah.

In summary, Rehoboam's downfall was precipitated by his arrogance, harshness, failure to listen to wise counsel, loss of support among the people, and inability to reconcile with the northern tribes, which ultimately weakened his rule and led to the division of the kingdom.

The unteachable spirit of a person in need of self-discipline.

The only thing that is constant is change. In this fast-paced world we live in, a good leader must always be open to learning new ways to build better relationships between the team and the customer. Therefore, leaders who fail to recognize this will fall into the trap of simply maintaining the status quo and, hence, moving backward in this regard. A teachable spirit will help leaders learn from their experiences, making it one of the most important leadership traits. If you fail to do so, then aligning your group with the company's actions will become challenging.

A person with an unteachable spirit often promotes a "know-it-all" attitude, which is seen as an element of pride. Such leaders may frequently interrupt conversations and demonstrate poor listening skills. This attitude shows a lack of self-control and causes the team to miss out on implementing great new ideas that are presented by others. Additionally, such a person lacks self-discipline. If a leader feels they are too big to do small things, then they are also too small to do big things for their team. You need to understand your strengths, weaknesses, and goals to be able to give your best self to your team and to have fulfillment.

Leaders need to be proactive, not just reactive. If you find yourself spending all your time trying to put out fires, then you aren't using your time effectively. Proactive leaders influence the future and form the right alliances to advance their causes. Of course, you should make sure your group is getting all the answers and resources they need, but don't ignore the future.

If you want to lead a team, you must constantly communicate with them and ensure they are all in the know. If you fail to communicate effectively, people won't know what to do next or where the group is heading.

Historical Perspective in Antiquity: It is said that God saw potential in Jeroboam to be a leader and ruler over the northern tribes of Israel. Jeroboam was chosen to fulfill this role after the kingdom split following Solomon's reign. God saw qualities in Jeroboam that made him suitable for leadership, such as his strength, leadership abilities, and perhaps a desire to serve the people. However, Jeroboam's downfall came when he turned away from following God's commands and embraced idolatry and disobedience instead. Jeroboam's downfall is primarily attributed in the Bible to his disobedience to God's commands. He was chosen by God to rule over the northern tribes of Israel after the kingdom split, but he turned away from God by instituting idolatry and leading the people into sin. He showed great promise, yet his egotistical "know it all" attitude forced him to make choices independent of God, resulting in various calamities, including the death of his son and the eventual destruction of his lineage.

Several years ago, as a young adult entering the workforce, I desperately yearned to live a life that was meaningful and rewarding not only financially but emotionally and psychologically as well. My parents and elders often advised me that life was about choices. In my heart, I knew that to find meaning; I needed to choose wisely along life's journey. However, my dilemma was this: If I suddenly came upon a fork in the road along life's journey, how would I know which road was the right one to take? Who could I trust to call for help, and if this person did help me, how could I be sure that their direction was flawless? How could anyone know ahead of time which pitfalls to avoid unless, of course, this person had trod this path already and knew firsthand where each path led?

Can a man or woman be so well-informed, experienced, and knowledgeable as to determine the truth one hundred percent of the time? If such a person did exist, would he or she be able to be approachable and available to anyone in times of desperate confusion and need? Impossible as it may seem, man has never found the answers to his problems by looking for them among the knowledgeable elite in our political, academic, or philosophical circles of learned men and women. It seemed to me that there was no certainty that the solutions lay in the minds of those solely because their intellectual fame outclassed our own.

Typically, in our desperate attempt to find someone dependable to trust, we tend to latch on to someone in our very own circle of life, someone who stands taller, smarter, more educated, wealthier, or more respected than others we know—anyone who seemed to be a cut above the rest. This person could be an older sibling, spouse, parent, neighbor, teacher, preacher, or friend. We compare their lifestyles, societal uprightness, and several other attributes until we feel assured that we can trust this person or

13

people to help us make the best choices for our own lives. Alas, it is never so easy.

Let me illustrate this with an example. I recall reading a story of a well-dressed man who used to go to work every day, and on his way, he would stop outside a clockmaker's store and synchronize his watch with the clock in the window. One day, the clockmaker stopped him and said, "I am amazed that every day you stop and synchronize your watch with my clock. What kind of work do you do?"

The man replied, "I am embarrassed to tell you this, but I'm the timekeeper at the factory, and the clocks in the factory don't work very well. So, I synchronize my watch with your clock every morning because I have to ring the bell at four o'clock every afternoon at the end of the day's shift."

The clockmaker started laughing and said, "You're not going to believe this. My clock doesn't work very well either. I synchronize it with the bell that I hear from the factory at four o'clock every afternoon."

What happens when two incorrect watches try to correct themselves by each other? They will become more and more out of sync with reality every single day.

The above humorous anecdote reminds us that, unfortunately, we mortals can be as blind as the ones we lead while still pretending to see.

What if there was someone human enough to understand human predicaments and yet divine enough to know what lies ahead as we journey through life? Can such a person exist? If they do exist, where can I find them? What available evidence can I find to end my search for a true leader, teacher, brother, and friend?

Chapter 2

A Matter of (Expert) Opinion

I knew that my search for such a charismatic leader must be based on and supported by strong evidence. I was not ready to compromise by following someone only to discover later that I was wrong. I did not want to place all my bets, hopes, and dreams on someone who is perhaps just a myth. I was sure I was not the only person in the world who wanted such a role model. Thus, I searched the library for books to learn the opinions of great scientists, historians, and philosophers on this subject.

My search for a logical and plausible answer drove me to explore the great minds of our world. My research amazed me as it narrowed down and pointed to someone who pursued his earthly calling for just about three short years, as recorded in the biblical gospels of the New Testament pertaining to the Christian worldview. Let us explore what modern scholars and historians have to say about Jesus. Was he a myth, or did a historical Jesus exist? If Jesus is a myth, we can put him in a bottle, like a genie, but if he is who he claims to be, we desperately need to seek him out. Without a strong, trusting, and caring leader, most of our lives will be like a ship without a compass, seemingly scalar in definition, where you may have a purpose but no sense of direction to get you where you want to be.

*Here is what **a renowned scientist** had to say: "I am a Jew, but I am enthralled by the luminous figure of the Nazarene. Jesus is too colossal for the pen of phrase mongers, however artful." He further added, "No man can read the Gospels without feeling the actual presence of Jesus. His personality pulsates in every word. No myth is filled with such life. Theseus and other heroes of his type lack the authentic vitality of Jesus."— **Albert Einstein, Scientist and Mathematician.**[7]*

I continued to search for evidence and found several convictions of some such well-known noble people in antiquity. I was amazed at the expert opinions on the subject, not just by scientists but even politicians like Napoleon Bonaparte: "I know men, and I tell you that Jesus Christ is no mere man. Between Him *and every other person in the world, there is no possible term of comparison. Alexander, Caesar, Charlemagne, and myself founded empires, but what foundation did we rest on the creations of our genius? Upon force. Jesus Christ founded an empire upon love, and at this hour millions of men would die for Him." — **Napoleon Bonaparte** (French General, Politician and Emperor (1804-14). 1769-1821). However, The earliest instance of that quote I could find was in the book "Our Christian Heritage" by James Gibbons, published in 1889, and he provides no source, which is a shame and a pain because he seems pretty good about sources otherwise.*

Allegedly, the quote appears in an earlier text dated 1845, "Sentiment de Napoleon sur la Divinite de Jesus Christ," by Robert-Augustin Antoine de Beauterne, but I cannot easily verify the contents, as it is in French.

*"A man who was completely innocent offered himself as a sacrifice for the good of others, including his enemies, and became the ransom of the world. It was a perfect act." — **Mahatma Gandhi,** Indian political leader (1869-1948)[8]*

A Scottish theologian summarized it best in his writings titled "The Strong Name."[9]

He was the meekest and lowliest of all the sons of men, yet he spoke of coming on the clouds of heaven with the glory of God. He was so austere that evil spirits and demons cried out in terror at his coming, yet he was so genial and winsome and approachable that children loved to play with him and the little ones nestled in his arms. His presence at the innocent joy of a village wedding was like the presence of sunshine. No one was nearly as kind or compassionate to sinners, yet no one ever spoke such red-hot, scorching words about sin. A bruised reed he would not break. His entire life was love. Yet, on one occasion, he demanded of the Pharisees how they expected to escape the damnation of hell.

He was a dreamer of dreams and a seer of visions, yet for sheer stark realism, he soundly beats all of us self-styled realists. He was the servant of all, washing the disciples' feet, yet masterfully, he strode into the temple, causing the hucksters and money changers to fall over one another to get away in their mad rush from the fire they saw blazing in his eyes. He saved others, yet ultimately, he did not save himself.

There is nothing in history like the union of contrasts which confronts us in the gospels; the mystery of Jesus is the mystery of divine personality" - **James Stewart**, *Scottish theologian.*

People from India, a country in South Asia, are unique in a particular way. It is home to people of numerous faiths, languages, and religions, such as Hinduism, Islam, Christianity, Sikhism, Buddhism, Jainism, and many others. The exact number varies depending on the categorization of different belief systems and sects, but hundreds of distinct faiths are practiced in India. In many of my conversations with young people, both around the kitchen table and in informal settings, I am often asked why Jesus is particularly considered more holier than leaders from other faiths? The general understanding is that all religions are the same, and they are simply different paths leading to nirvana, moksha, or what we understand as salvation. Jesus, too, in his time, was considered a "mere" good man like all other prophets. However, mere goodness was by no means sufficient to explain him. Moreover, the historical setting in which he grew up, the psychological mood and temper of the age and the house of Israel, and the economic and social predicament of Jesus' family—all these attributes were considered normal. However, the moment he asserted being one with the Father in heaven, they threw stones at him. Our questions, too, even in today's age, fail to answer one significant question: Why does he differ from all others in the same setting?

In Christianity, salvation is often seen as a gift from God, granted through faith in Jesus Christ rather than earned through merit or good deeds. This perspective is rooted in the belief that humans are inherently flawed and incapable of earning salvation through their own merits. Instead, Christians believe that salvation is a result of God's grace and forgiveness, freely offered to all who accept Jesus as their savior. Other religions may have different views on salvation, often based on a combination of faith, deeds, and *adherence to religious laws or teachings. Superficially, all religions may seem the same, but fundamentally, they differ significantly from the message delivered by Jesus Christ. In the Gospel of John 14:**6**, Jesus said to him, "I am the way, and the truth, and the life; no one comes to the Father but by me."[10] In other words, this is a call to develop a relationship with him, and in doing so, good deeds will spring from your heart, not just from your requirement to merit His salvation. This uniqueness in the spiritual life of Jesus has led Christians to see Him not only as a human being but as one encompassed by divinity.*

*On the other hand, what about those people of great stature in the scientific community who hold opposite opinions? Let's consider the worldview of **Stephen Hawking,** who was widely acclaimed as one of the most brilliant minds in the world. This is what he had to say: "What I have done is to show that it is possible for the way the universe began to be determined by the laws of science. In that case, it would not be necessary to appeal to God to decide how the universe began. This doesn't prove that there is no God, only that God is not necessary."[11] (Der Spiegel, October 17, 1988)*

Renowned Biologist and atheist Richard Dawkins has said, "In a universe of electrons and selfish genes, blind physical forces and genetic replication, some people are going to get hurt, other people are going to get lucky, and you won't find any rhyme or reason in it, nor any justice. The universe that we observe has precisely the properties we should expect if there is, at the bottom, no design, no purpose, no evil, no good, nothing but pitiless indifference."[12] Dawkins stated that things were not a freak accident. He explained that Darwin demonstrated it happened through evolution by natural selection. He said it looks designed, but it is not. He said that the cosmos has not had its 'Darwin' yet, so we do not know how it was created. He asserted that biology could discourage us from believing in God. He claimed that although we don't understand the cosmos, we do not have to postulate a creator. He says it's harder to think of how a God came into existence than a universe.[13]

The Atheist's explanation of how the world began is postulated by the theory of the "Big Bang," with the sun, exploding stars, and other cosmic catastrophes flooding the universe and slipping through walls and our bodies by the billions every second like the evening sunlight through a screen of a sliding door.

The Big Bang Theory is a scientific model explaining the origin and evolution of the universe. It proposes that the universe began as a singularity—an extremely hot and dense point, about 13.8 billion years ago. From this singularity, the universe rapidly expanded and continues to expand today. This theory is supported by various pieces of evidence and observations, such as the cosmic microwave background radiation and the observed expansion of the universe. The Big Bang Theory is supported by a vast amount of evidence from multiple scientific disciplines, including astronomy, physics, and cosmology. However, science doesn't prove theories in the same way mathematical theorems are proven. Instead, scientific theories are supported by evidence and continually tested and refined through observation, experimentation, and analysis. The Big Bang Theory has withstood extensive scrutiny and is widely accepted within the scientific community as the most plausible explanation for the origin and evolution of the universe.

Chapter 3

Science or God

Did the Big Bang Theory Decimate God?

"Only two things are infinite, the universe and human stupidity, and I'm not sure about the universe."[14]—Albert Einstein.

At the outset, it is important to clarify that the Bible is not a book of science. The Bible is primarily a religious and historical text that contains stories, teachings, and moral guidance. While it may touch on aspects of the natural world, its primary focus is not scientific explanations or discoveries. The Bible is a historical document that describes God's plan of salvation for fallen mankind.

When asked about the greatest of all his amazing accomplishments, Sir Isaac Newton cited the discovery of gravity. He said it helped him keep his feet on the ground and strengthened his faith in a creator. He further stated that this most beautiful system of the sun, planets, and comets could only proceed from the counsel and dominion of an intelligent Being. This Being governs all things, not as the soul of the world, but as Lord over all, and on account of his dominion, he is wont to be called "Lord God" or "Universal Ruler." The Supreme God is a Being eternal, infinite, [and] absolutely perfect.[15]

It was a warm afternoon in August 2020, and we were simply enjoying our daughter Nicole's sudden visit. Nicole and my son Randolph often delight us with such visits, and my wife Sandra and I love sitting around, talking, and exchanging pleasant memories with them. Very often, we spend time basking in each other's company while sitting around a patio table in the backyard of our home in Toronto, Canada. Invariably, you will find us sipping freshly squeezed lemonade as we chat and nibble on some crackers and cheese. It was Nicole's idea that I should mention Science and God in this book. I thought it was an excellent idea, and thus, this chapter of my book was born that day.

Having spent my entire working life in the field of Engineering, I have become so accustomed to applying scientific laws and theories to determine technical outcomes. Many of us are *quite familiar with some common examples of laws named after people, such as Darcy's law in fluid mechanics, Ampere's electromagnetic circuit laws in Physics, Dalton's law, Bell's Theorem, and Boltzmann Equations in Thermodynamics, Newton's laws of Gravity, Gay-Lussac's law in Chemistry, and others. Additionally, during the global COVID-19 pandemic, we encounter several conversations with family and friends around the kitchen table, wanting to stop and discuss some of life's difficult questions related to **origin**, **meaning**, **morality,** and **destiny**. This leads to further discussions about other laws, such as Hubble's Law in Cosmology, Mendel's Laws in Genetics, Kepler's Law of planetary motion, and the list goes on.*

Wikipedia states, "Some laws reflect mathematical symmetries found in Nature (e.g., the Pauli Exclusion Principle reflects the identity of electrons, conservation laws reflect homogeneity of space, time, and Lorentz transformations reflect rotational symmetry of space-time). Many fundamental physical laws are mathematical consequences of various symmetries of space, time, or other aspects of nature.

Scientific laws summarize the results of experiments or observations, usually within a certain range of application. The nature of scientific laws has been much discussed in philosophy, but in essence, scientific laws are simply empirical conclusions reached by the scientific method; they are intended to be laden neither with ontological commitments nor with statements of logical absolutes."[16]

Machines are dependent on and controlled by various applicable scientific laws. My entire working life has revolved around science and its application to life, in general, but I have never stopped asking the question: How did these laws come about in the first place? I realized that none of these laws were invented by the people after whom they were named, but every law was discovered. All the names associated with scientific laws were indeed seekers of explanations who found what they believed existed in nature.

C. S. Lewis sums it up well when he says, "Men became scientific because they expected law in nature, and they expected law in nature because they believed in a Legislator (lawgiver)."[17]

It becomes obvious, then, that we need to consider not just the various laws of science but also laws that pre-existed in the makings of the universe that we live in. This is the study of Natural law. Let us consider Energy, for example. The Sun is the source of energy for most life on Earth. It derives its energy mainly from nuclear fusion in its core converting mass to energy as protons are combined to form helium. This energy is transported to the sun's surface and then released into space, mainly in the form of radiant (light) energy. . The laws that govern how much energy is available are called the laws of thermodynamics and involve a concept known as entropy for irreversible thermodynamic processes. Yet the scientific world still cannot tell us what energy is!

Noted scientist Richard Feynman explains thus: "It is important to realize that in physics today, we have no knowledge of what energy is." We do not have a picture that energy exists in little blobs of a definite amount. It is not that way. It does not tell us the mechanism or the reason for the various formulas."[18] The world of pure academia asks us to choose between Science and God, but I postulate the question: Can Science live without God? Discoverers of various scientific laws believed in law and order in the universe, so they went out to look for it and discovered these laws. These great men and women of our world could practice Science only because they believed that there were precise sets of law and order that governed our universe. They believed in a lawgiver and in a mind behind creation.

Sir Isaac Newton's view has been close to deism and several biographers and scholars have labeled him as a deist who is strongly influenced by Christianity. However, he differed from strict adherents of deism in that he invoked God as a special physical cause to keep the planets in their orbit. He warned against using the law of gravity to view the universe as a mere machine, like a great clock. He said: "This most beautiful system of the sun, planets, and comets could only proceed from the counsel and dominion of an intelligent Being. This Being governs all things, not as the soul of the world, but as Lord over all, and on account of his dominion, he is wont to be called "Lord God" or "Universal Ruler."[19]

I further add that perhaps we need to consider very seriously that in the process of unraveling the mysteries of science, we just may discover the ultimate evidence of the eternal existence of GOD and the mystery of His being. I am convinced that the question need not be science or God. Perhaps we will be equally amazed to find out that the BIG BANG was simply the sound of GOD at work, hammering out this magnificent universe we live in.

Historical evidence shows that Science and God coexist. I suggest a pause while you contemplate which of the three mathematical equations are empirically veritable:

Science – (minus) God = BIG BANG?

Science – (minus) BIG BANG = GOD?

*I urge you to pause and consider the evidence: **SCIENCE = GOD + (plus) BIG BANG.***

Chapter 4

Gain Altitude by Your Attitude

My excitement grew day by day as I read more about this newly found teacher, called Jesus, the Nazarene. As a young person entering the workforce, I attempted to separate the profound lessons in leadership that intrigued me, yet I was not ready to blindly accept the Christian worldview of God's plan of salvation. I was more interested in leadership skills, whether radical or not, that would help me in my work and satisfy my ambitions to be the best I could be. In my heart, I knew that financial and material success came from emulating work habits from the best and then going into my workplace and proving my abilities. Moreover, I knew that learning

from the best implies deliberate acceptance, intellectual assent, and a conviction that applies to a firmly and seriously held belief. Simply put: Belief is something that you hold, but conviction is that which holds you. I would rather have the latter.

Since this chapter is dedicated to finding evidence of the truth about the kind of example that Jesus presents, it is important to consult scholarly sources that are outside of the Christian worldview. My intention was to be completely objective and unbiased just because I was born in a Christian home. If He is a myth, let's put Him in a bottle and place Him on the shelf right next to Russell's teapot[20] and move onwards with my search. However, if evidence proves that Jesus is who he claims to be and does, in fact, have both human and divine natures, then we need to bottle up our agnosticism and cork away our doubts. The truth about the existence of the world's first revolutionary and radical teacher and leader was more important to me than mere worldviews. Little did I know at the time that separating the human Jesus from His divine nature would be difficult. I was open to understanding the Christian worldview at its core if that's what was needed to grasp the truth.

I began to read a portion of the New Testament of the Christian Bible daily, hoping that the words of one who claims to be human and also divine may pulsate in my mind.

"Jesus was not a white man; He was not a black man. He came from that part of the world that touches Africa, Asia, and Europe. Christianity is not a white man's religion, and don't let anybody ever tell you that it's white or black. Christ belongs to all people; He belongs to the whole world."[21] — Billy Graham (Christian evangelist).

Our hearts, minds, and souls combine emotional, logical, and spiritual evaluations of alternative responses to a stimulus, enabling us to choose our preferred approach. I learned that the presence of the Holy Spirit within a Christian's heart can bring God's wisdom to influence our choice of response if we let Him. This means that we move from being victims of the situations and circumstances that come our way to becoming empowered human beings filled with God's Spirit, who can turn all things into good.

Good leadership is intrinsically proactive in making decisions about where the organization is heading and how it will respond to the challenges faced along the way. Good leaders are not only proactive themselves but also foster a proactive attitude within the organization. Those who hold to the notion that only science can make truth claims fail to recognize that there are many realms of truth where science is impotent. For example:

• Science cannot prove the disciplines of mathematics and logic because it presupposes them.

• *Science cannot prove metaphysical truths such as minds, morals, and ethics. For example, science cannot be used to prove that the suicide bombers of 9/11 who flew their planes into the World trade tower were evil.*

• *Science is incapable of stating truths about the beauty of the rainbow, the setting sun, or the love of a mother for a child. Nor can science test any such philosophical claims.*

And there are those who say that absolute truth does not apply to morality. Yet, the response to the question: Is it morally acceptable to engage in suicide bombings that harm innocent people, kill children, or expect infidelity in a marriage? The answer to these queries is always a resounding "NO."

Leadership requires authority and power, both of which are loaded terms. In this world of political correctness, how does a leader lead, knowing that the multi-cultural folks they are leading may be suspicious of their motives in the face of their Christian beliefs?

For a Christian leader, it is important to know that you are not alone. Every day, you march to the beat of the very essence of a caring and loving creator. In and through the epitome of HIS omnipotence, I have experienced many overwhelming setbacks that have been transformed into set-ups for the greater good. I have grown to trust Him and find immense comfort in knowing that it is not important who you are but *"whose"* you are!

Everyone wants to feel appreciated

I recall an encounter with an employee during my transfer to a sister division within the greater Toronto area. Being new to this division, I was just getting to know everyone. Charlie was a big, burly man with arm muscles that would be the envy of a prizefighter. He was also our main machine operator and the best at his job. However, his interaction with people within our workplace had grown noticeably aggressive, and his language had become increasingly abusive and abrasive. Managers complained that the company's policy was zero tolerance for any sort of unruly behavior. I decided to counsel him privately in my office on one such occasion. The day of our meeting was set; he arrived at my office, walked up to my desk, and without saying a word, he settled down in the chair in front of me. I could tell from his demeanor that he bristled at the very idea of being there. The meeting turned out to be a disaster, and he left my office in a huff. In the days that followed, I noticed that he preferred to keep a physical distance from me whenever I toured the Factory floor.

Several weeks later, on a Monday morning, all hell broke loose. The production manager was distraught that we would not meet the customer's ship date since Charlie was producing parts *that consistently failed Quality control, and four hours into his shift, he was well below acceptable limits for no apparent reason. Therefore, Charlie was once more in my office. Looking through the glass window, I could almost predict the outcome, so I tried a different approach. I asked him to walk with me toward his machine, and we talked as we walked. I noticed that he constantly looked at his wristwatch, so I turned to face him and said, "Charlie, to me, work is important, and so are customer ship dates, but how you feel today is more important to me. Is there anything I can do to help you, Charlie?" His face softened up, and I could see that he was trying to control his emotions. Then he said something that stopped me in my tracks. He revealed that his 8-year-old son was ill, and the doctor suspected it was serious. He was expecting a call from the hospital about the diagnosis and was afraid the news would be devastating.*

He wished he could be at the hospital himself, but his car had broken down. So, that afternoon, I drove him to the hospital myself, and the doctor put all his fears to rest—his son was out of danger. I put all my meetings on hold that afternoon, did my best to put his mind at ease, and then we went for lunch. I recall the parable of the Lost Sheep, the wonderful story told by Jesus to illustrate the love and compassion that God has for everyone in His care.

Several days after this incident, I noticed a tremendous positive change in Charlie's behavior, and once again proved to be an asset to the organization. Remarkably, all it took was that Charlie needed to believe that we valued him as a person, and not just a productive worker on the factory floor.

*Roy T Bennett provides a concise list of ways that are effective morale boosters, but "only **if they are expressed with a genuine spirit:***

1. *Use their name.*
2. *Express sincere gratitude.*
3. *Do more listening than talking.*
4. *Talk more about them than about you.*
5. *Be authentically interested.*
6. *Be sincere in your praise.*
7. *Show you care. "[22]*

*These seven great points are nice to consider and use on a daily basis; however, the words that stand out are "**If they are expressed with a genuine spirit.**" Words come from the mouth, but genuine words emerge from the heart. People recognize the spirit in which you communicate; it's also not what you say but how you say it. Nothing can replace the tone of your voice, your attention, and your ability to just listen without prejudging. Listening is a skill which we will continue to explore further along.*

Obviously, the answer does not solely depend on "simply hiring the best," although I agree that it does set up a stronger basis on which a relationship is established, nurtured, and maintained.

The secret of Jesus' ability to constantly rise above the circumstances lies in two things: **Firstly**, *He developed a relationship with HIS father in heaven, who was HIS "point of reference," the fulcrum of His faith and the author and source of life.* **Secondly**, *He never took His eye off the goal and purpose, i.e., to save His people from the wages of sin, which is eternal separation from God. In other words, and yet what was even more important to Jesus was his journey and his interaction during his very short ministry. Jesus' life took on two dimensions:* **the vertical dimension** *in relationship with His Father in heaven* **and the horizontal dimension** *of unconditional love for all of God's people, especially the ones who caused Him the most pain. The cross is a great reminder of these two dimensions, and while He still hung there, we can still hear His prayer for us: "Father, forgive them, for they know not what they do."*[23]

As workplace supervisors and managers, we sooner or later encounter certain individuals with a particular aspect of their personality and manner that seems to become quite unnerving and abrasive. The instant reaction one experiences is irritability and a desire to "show" him who the boss is. If you fail to put this in perspective, this irritability can turn to dislike and even enmity over time. It takes just one contumelious individual to breed disdain and discontent among the rest of the team. However, this individual also acts as a messenger, sending out a message of scorn and contempt. Try to understand the message; maybe you will find a lesson to learn and possibly understand the messenger.

Lesson learned: "A person who feels appreciated puts out more than what is expected of him or her."[24]

Chapter 5

A Testimony: Seeking a Leader, Finding a Fisherman (More Accurately, A Fisher of Men).

———✺———

In the early days of my career, I was alone, far from the country of my birth. It was one of those scorching summer days in Kuwait, a Middle Eastern country, with temperatures reaching fifty degrees Celsius and above, and on such days, you could literally fry an egg on the sidewalk. On a blistering day such as this, I accidentally bumped into an old friend, Michael Bunyan (his real name). We talked about various things, primarily about what was going on in our lives. I learned that Mike had moved up the corporate ladder at his place of work and was doing very well. He shared his own experiences about work and family, which I found quite interesting. Then Mike invited me to share a meal with him, and just before we ate, he said a short prayer. I was a bit taken aback by the sincerity of his prayer. Well, I had heard of "holy Joe" but not "holy Mike." Later that week, Mike invited me to attend a prayer meeting at his local church. Since I had already committed to meeting up with friends, I very politely declined. A few weeks had passed by since my meeting with Mike, who continued to keep in touch over the phone. It was Thursday, and I was excitedly making plans for the upcoming weekend party with friends, and then the phone rang...

It was devastating news from home about the sudden tragic death of my brother-in-law. This news left my widowed sister with a 4-year-old daughter grief-stricken and flummoxed. Memories came flooding about my older sister, who I remembered as the smartest and most hardworking among us seven siblings. Growing up, she was my math teacher, always ready to help me with my studies. She excelled in school and was allowed to skip grades in Junior high due to her ability to hold consistently high scores in all subjects. The news of her husband's death was unexpected and left me helpless.

I paced the floor of my apartment, feeling as though I were in the middle of a crowded room with no one there but myself. It was suffocating. It was noon when the phone rang, and it was Mike on the other end of the line. Before I could relate the sad news, he said,

"Hey Newton, would you like to join me for a prayer meeting tomorrow evening?" It felt like his words offered me hope, which at the moment in time seemed like a lone candle in a dark cave, flickering against the shadows and refusing to be extinguished. Amidst my anguish, I suddenly felt a tad bit more hopeful and seemed to discover a faint glow of possibility, illuminating a path forward through the caverns of uncertainty. It took a few moments to respond to Mike, which seemed like an eternity. I agreed to go with him to the prayer meeting the next day.

OUT OF EVERY TRAGEDY COMES NEW STRENGTH. *"Tragedy is like strong acid; it dissolves away all but the very gold of truth."[25]*

The prayer meeting consisted of about 30 people of mixed backgrounds and a various age group. I was charmed by the simplicity of the intercessory prayer of the people that evening. Although I was born in a Catholic home, I admit that the world and all its charms gradually led me to drift away from the shores of my Christian faith, like a leaf carried by the currents of doubt and introspection. Each moment of questioning was a gentle tug, pulling me further from the comfort of familiar beliefs until I found myself adrift in a sea of uncertainty, grappling with the waves of conflicting ideologies and personal revelations. Here I was now, in a strange room, navigating the uncharted waters of my spiritual journey. Upon reaching home, I slumped on my bed, nursing a very troubled conscience. I asked myself, what is it that makes people bring out their problems in prayer before strangers? Was it desperation, was it confidence among friends, or was it simple childlike faith in a real creator?

The seed of desire to know this faith can be deeply personal and subjective. Over the next few weeks, I found myself yearning for a deeper connection with something greater than me. I felt an emptiness within me that craved spiritual fulfillment. I felt a longing in my soul for a sense of purpose and meaning coupled with a hunger for faith to guide me through life's uncertainties. I sought solace and comfort in the embrace of a higher power, and my heart ached for a faith that could provide me with strength and hope. I wondered what it must be like to have a deep desire to explore and nurture my spiritual beliefs. Over the following weeks, as I attended weekly prayer meetings, I was drawn to the idea of surrendering to a divine presence beyond my understanding. There was a longing within me that only faith could satisfy. I also yearned for a profound need to cultivate a deeper relationship with my spirituality.

Through Mike's unshakeable faith, I began to feel a zest and a brand-new perspective on life. I marveled at his knowledge and interpretation of biblical passages. I learned fast as my need to know this Jesus grew stronger each day. We were strangers, my new King James Bible and me. The language seemed ancient, almost poetic at times, and the verses were hard to comprehend. I began to realize that what started as only a seed was now germinating and growing. My initial search for simply a great leadership role model had now deeply mingled with the understanding of Jesus' divinity.

Then after a couple of weeks, my initial ardor began to decline as my lukewarm faith started to grow cold as I neglected reading daily scripture passages. The distractions and temptations of the world can often lead one away from your spiritual path. Mike came to my rescue once again; he mentored me and reminded me that I needed to spend more time in prayer and meditation each day to cultivate a deeper connection with the divine. He urged me to regularly read and study sacred texts of the Bible and even suggested appropriate chapters to read, which gave me an understanding of the passages and also the chronological events that followed the teachings of Jesus and his chosen apostles and various letters written to the churches even after the crucifixion of Jesus. I knew I needed to actively participate during Spiritual Gatherings as well as join a community of like-minded individuals through attending religious services, study groups, or spiritual retreats. This shift helped me focus less on just myself and more on cultivating an attitude of gratitude by reflecting on the blessings in my life and acknowledging the presence of the divine. I found myself taking time to reflect on my shortcomings, which were many, or areas where I stray easily, and seek forgiveness through repentance.

Once again, I started surrounding myself with supportive individuals who share their spiritual values and aspirations.

In the depths of my soul, I ached for further evidence, a celestial whisper, a divine revelation—to confirm the existence of a personal God. Before leaving for the prayer meeting that Thursday evening, I knelt on my knees and spoke my heart out to God, telling him that if He was real, then He should answer my quest for divine assurance. I prayed to seek the footprints of the divine in the tapestry of my earthly existence and asked for a sign that would affirm His existence. I had read a story of Gideon's fleece found in the book of Judges, chapter 6, in the Old Testament of the Bible. Gideon came from the weakest clan in Israel; even his father worshipped idols, so he wanted reassurance that the Lord wanted him to lead. He was uncertain about God's plan for him and asked for a sign. He placed a fleece, a piece of wool, on the threshing floor and asked God to make it wet with dew while keeping the ground dry. God granted his request. Then, Gideon asked for the opposite sign, and God fulfilled it as well, strengthening Gideon's faith and resolve. I wanted to see something just as convincing, so that evening in April, I made a seemingly sincere but kind of childish pact with God.

I took my study chair and turned it upside down, locked the door to my room, and prayed that if God was really who the Bible claimed Him to be, then I would like to see the chair arranged right side up upon my return. I then left for the prayer meeting. At the prayer meeting, right in the midst of the time allotted for meditation, Mike laid his hand on my shoulder and prayed for the outpouring of the Holy Spirit upon me. His request seemed presumptuous and impulsive. I closed my eyes more out of embarrassment and feeling sorry for Mike and his expectant faith. A passage of scripture that I read earlier instantly came to mind from the gospel of Matthew. "Or what man is there of you, whom if his son asks bread, will he give him a stone? Or if he asks a fish, will he give him a serpent? If ye then, being evil, know how to give good gifts unto your children, how much more shall your Father which is in heaven give good things to them that ask him?"[26]

I felt the need to pray, so I said these words: "Oh God, I am unworthy to receive beautiful gifts from you. My heart will rejoice if only I am certain that you are real". In that instant, my senses numbed, and my mind blanked. It was a strong and unique sensation, and I felt blessed. It was a moment of indescribable peace; it drained all my energy, and my eyes were overflowing with what seemed like an unending stream of tears of repentance. I found myself saying the words, "Who is like unto you, O Lord." At the end of the evening, I reached home and couldn't wait to open the door of my room to see if my "Gideon's fleece" actually worked. But nothing happened: the chair I had turned upside down was exactly as I had left it. I related this childish incident to Mike and wondered why God had not answered my request just as He did with Gideon.

I could hear Mike chuckling away on the phone, and he said that God was more interested in turning your life right side up!! Of course, he was right again. I now understand that God desires our lives to be upright because living in alignment with moral principles and righteousness brings harmony, justice, and goodness to the world. Upholding upright lives fosters love, compassion, and respect for others, leading to stronger communities and deeper connections with the divine. It also allows individuals to fulfill their potential and live purposeful, fulfilling lives. Ultimately, God's desire for upright living reflects His love for humanity and His vision for a better world.

I am reminded of the passage I read in the Book of Jeremiah 29:13 - "And ye shall seek me, and find me when ye shall search for me with all your heart."[27]

TODAY: My God is a God of compassion and slow to anger. He pours out new and tangible proof of His love every day. Am I perceptible enough, or am I like those who have eyes but do not see? Some may call my testimony foolish, others skeptical, and yet others may call me superficial. I realize that the fear of understanding God's ways with an intellectual mind alone cripples my heart. The crudest form of fear is when we are ashamed to speak of Jesus, the King of Kings, the Lord of Lords, the Fisher of Men and Women, just because others may not appreciate it. I remember the moment God allowed His love to flow even on little old me, a lost sheep in

His fold. How can I deny the fleeting treasure I held? What an utter joy to share, so excellent is His altar call.

Human behavior is still profoundly influenced by our intrinsic desires and impulses. The choices we face are often a testament to the internal conflicts between our conscious values and unconscious drives. In the tapestry of human existence, the threads of sin and virtue are woven together. Our journey is marked by the constant interplay of these forces, shaping the choices we make and the lives we lead. Each of us wrestles with our own imperfections and moral challenges. The decisions we make daily reflect our ongoing struggle to overcome our sinful inclinations and strive for better. Hence, we ought to be open to learning, and this calls for humility and deep introspection.

As Jesus offers us new brothers and sisters in Christ, yet in my heart, I reflect on the passage in 1 Corinthians 4:15 King James Version (KJV)

"For though ye have ten thousand instructors in Christ, yet have ye, not many fathers: for in Christ Jesus I have begotten you through the gospel."

I now realize why it is impossible to separate the human Jesus from his divine self. The answer lies in the vertical and horizontal dimensions of the Cross. The vertical dimension of the Cross signifies that without God's mercy, compassion, and strength,

49

we cannot apply the horizontal dimension of the same Cross, which involves serving and loving all people. As mentioned earlier, we ought to constantly remember that God expects us to understand the parable of the "Good Samaritan," as mentioned in the story told in Luke 10:29–37: A man going from Jerusalem to Jericho is attacked by robbers who strip him and beat him. A priest and a Levite pass by without helping him. But a Samaritan stops to care for him, taking him to an inn where the Samaritan pays for his care.

Matthew 25:35-40 KJV summarizes this: "Whatsoever you do unto the least of my brothers, you do unto me, says the Lord."

We measure God's love for us when we look at the cross of Christ; God measures our love for HIM by looking down the "Jericho" road.

Lesson learned: **A true leader inspires followers to become greater leaders than himself.**

Chapter 6

Setting Realistic Goals & Leadership Styles

*ANYONE CAN MANAGE. "The first responsibility of a leader is to define reality. The last is to say thank you. In between the two, the leader must become a **servant and a debtor**. That sums up the progress of an artful leader."[28]—Max De Pree.*

In the latter part of the year, when Generation Z was just preparing to get a foot in the workforce, I was dedicating my time as a Business Management consultant to other divisions of our parent company in foreign lands. Around this time, I was brought into a conversation with the Vice President of the company regarding the state of matters in one of our many worldwide divisions. Despite several attempts to restore the financial situation of this business, the operating income of this particular division was in the negative and had been so for at least the past five years. Plans were in place to cut our losses, sell off this acquisition, and move on. However, as a last resort, I was requested to devote all my attention to doing everything I could to revive it before they pulled the plug on this entity.

The very first thing I remember doing upon arriving home was to go to the throne before I went to the phone. I repeated the words uttered by Solomon when he was given the empire:

1. *I thanked God for the past and all that He bestowed upon my family and me.*
2. *I admitted my frailties and inabilities with all humility*
3. *I admitted my fears and was completely dependent on God's favor.*

The long and short of it is that my team and I managed to pull this division out of the financial distress in just two short years. We not only surpassed the company's expectations financially but also nurtured a team of fine, dependable and capable men and women. A lesson to be learned is that while one may be employed at one of the best Fortune 500 companies, the person you report to on a daily basis is the one who daily represents the organization as well. Therefore, lead well with fairness, consistency, honesty, and respect at all times.

Our Lord and Savior understands the need for money in our lives, just as he did by helping his foster father, Joseph, through the fine craft of carpentry. Jesus reminds us that we must give unto Caesar what belongs to Caesar and give unto God what belongs to God. However, we are reminded that the love of money is a root of all kinds of evil, and in their eagerness to be rich, some have wandered away from the faith and pierced themselves with many pains. (1 Timothy 6:10 NRSV).

My quest and thirst to know more about the Christian worldview, in particular, helped me to realize that Jesus set a new and radical standard of leadership. He was the natural leader. He did not have to raise His voice or strike the synagogue pulpit to be heard. When He entered the room, a hush fell over the people. He was a born leader. Jesus grew in favor with God and with men and women (Luke 2:52). He went around doing good (Acts 10:38). The common people heard Him gladly. He spoke with authority, unlike the Scribes and the Pharisees (Matthew 7:29). The Apostle Paul often wrote about the "grace of our Lord Jesus Christ" (2 Corinthians 8:9). He was such an attractive person that people were drawn to Him like iron filings to a magnet (Luke 4:15).

How does a Christian leader who understands the monotheist storyline — creation, fall, redemption, resurrection — then understand what he does on a regular Monday morning in relation to that grand metanarrative in a secular place of work?

The world's first Managers: Adam and Eve

My mind drifts to a story I once read in the Book of Genesis, the first book of the Bible. God had a garden that needed to be taken care of, and so HE not just hired but fashioned his first two employees, Adam & Eve, from dust and bone, giving them some specific rules and policies to upkeep. He also empowered them with the responsibility for this garden and the freedom of choice. There were no requirements for Health, Safety, or environmental issues since they were to manage a perfectly planned and well-balanced ecological haven.

God said, "I give you every seed-bearing plant on the face of the whole earth and every tree that has fruit with seed in it. They will be yours for food."[29] (Gen 1:29). Adam could be known as our world's first real "Plant Manager" and Eve having been given equal status, together they named each plant, tree, fruit, and animal, filing it away in memory. We know this as a branch of science concerned with classification, especially of organisms.

Everything seemed productive and easy until another entity (a talking serpent) questioned the rules and the policies that were already in place. The Garden of Eden did not go bankrupt, claim insolvency, or lose to the prevailing competition, but rather closed doors due to problems related to conflicting ideas, overbearing influence, wavering trust, and hence the inability to make the right choice.

Undoubtedly, the responsibility of managing a business involves the ability to enforce an organization's rules, policies, and procedures. However, when it comes to people, a successful manager must seek to lead, not manage. Leadership style is the manner and approach used to provide direction, implement plans, and motivate people.

"Wealth can be gained, but financial health must be maintained. What does it profit a man to gain great wealth but in the process lose financial health."[30]—author of this book.

Any Organization requires a leader or Manager to focus on providing the best of two things:

1. *Profitability – using tangible skills.*

2. *Culture within the organization – using people skills*

The purpose of any Business is PROFITABILITY

Definition: *"Profitability is the ability of a company to use its resources to generate revenues more than its expenses. In other* *words, this is a company's capability of generating profits from its operations".*

Profitability is one of four building blocks for analyzing financial statements and company performance. The other three are efficiency, solvency, and market prospects. Investors, creditors, and managers use these key concepts to analyze how well a company is performing and the potential it could reach in a productive and efficient operation.[31]

The two key aspects of profitability are revenues and expenses. Revenues are the business income. This is the amount of money earned from customers by selling products or providing services. However, generating income is not free. Businesses must utilize their resources to produce these products and provide these services.

*In a nutshell, a good leader understands that profitability is a two-sided coin: on the one hand, looms the mammoth effort needed to **maximize** revenue or **sales**, and on the other hand, it demands a great deal of creativity and continuous improvement effort that is needed in creating a lean and efficient enterprise, in order to **minimize** the **cost** of those Sales.*

What is a GREAT workplace CULTURE?

Many authors have written about the importance of having a great workplace culture. This raises the most obvious question:

what does a great culture look like? Aside from benefits, great snacks, and funky office decorations, there are many more important fundamentals that must be in place to build a positive environment where employees can be most productive and engaged.

On work ethic:

Nobody should feel like a cog in some huge machine, performing habitual and routine tasks with no meaning. It certainly does not mean that a mission statement needs to be memorized for an upcoming Quality audit; it means they should know how their daily work is affecting the company's performance.

A great company aims to hire people who can fit into its culture. Diversity is extremely important. I have often heard the phrase, "There is unity in diversity." This means that each one brings their uniqueness and together form a common work ethic and feel comfortable in the company's environment. Hiring a person accustomed to working in a highly different environment needs to be prepared to assimilate and willing to change in order to fit in with the rest.

A <u>great company culture creates a collaborative environment</u> where everyone works toward a common vision for the organization rather than solely looking out for themselves. When people hoard information or try to compete with others to get ahead, *it signifies a toxic culture. This kind of self-serving behavior must not be encouraged.*

What does it mean in philosophical terms?

Philosophically, from a biblical perspective, there are three forms of culture. Human beings interact using these forms, irrespective of happenstance, whether in the context of a country, a home, or a workplace.

According to Ravi Zacharias, there are three kinds of culture: "Theonomous, Heteronomous, and Autonomous."[32]

Theonomous *is not a theocracy; "Theos" means God, and "nomos" means law. In a theonomous culture, the idea is that God's law is self-evident within the human heart. It becomes obvious that there are some imperatives within you that reach a consensus in society. This is synonymous with a democratic style where a framework or expectation is provided to guide the masses, where the participants are encouraged to make choices that are aligned and draw their actions to coincide within the framework of those expectations.*

*In a **Heteronomous culture**, the mainstream of the culture is dictated by the leadership at the top. This culture is a form of authoritative or autocratic style where every aspect is dictated and controlled by a few leaders in a top-down leadership. This may seem* *to work from the outside, but it lacks heartfelt involvement, and hence, it can end up being a practice based on fear and retribution.*

*An **Autonomous culture** is where free reign is encouraged. Some benefits of such a culture are that you play a part in making the contributions you offer meaningful and authentic. The more potential risk a type of autonomy carries for the organization, the more meaningful it becomes to the employee. In other words, giving employees the freedom to decorate their cubicles while directing their team activities with an iron fist means nothing. It's an insult. At times, meaningful autonomy may mean that the boss trusts you with something that has the potential to embarrass the organization or cost it money, making you much more likely to handle things with care. However, if the organization's culture does not support the processes that self-managed teams require, you must also be aware of some of the pitfalls, too:*

- *A concept of groupthink may take over, where individuals' ideas are put on the back burner in favor of conformity to team norms.*

- *Creative thoughts may be smothered as team members knuckle down to support others' ideas.*

- *Some team members may see it as a step too far and desire more management intervention.*

- *Fear-based decisions may inhibit free thinking and progressive risk-taking.*

- *Too many team members may slow down decision-making, as there needs to be consensus between members. The management hierarchy might feel pushed out and want more involvement in making decisions and reaching conclusions. This is another extreme where this is not a style to use so that you can blame others when things go wrong; rather, this is a style to be used when you fully trust and develop confidence in the people below you. In short, a situation where "everybody is right, and nobody is wrong" does not align with the paradigm that expects accountability and discipline.*

This songwriter warns us in the lyrics of a verse by rock musician King Crimson:

> *"Knowledge is a deadly friend*
>
> *When no one sets the rules.*
>
> *The fate of all mankind, I see*
>
> *Is in the hands of fools."*

In order for workplace culture to bear good fruit, must it tie into workplace leadership styles?

Yes, it must adopt the best or a suitable combination of the three major styles of leadership, which are:

- *Participative or democratic*

- *Delegated or Free Reign*

- *Authoritarian or autocratic*

The purpose of this book is twofold: **Firstly**, *to crystallize all the various styles of Leadership out there into one simple yet effective style that I have personally used successfully over the last 30 years.* **Secondly**, *it provides a Christian perspective as a foundation upon which one can build a rewarding career and, at the same time, build valued relationships in the process.*

Therefore, for the purpose of simplification, I will attempt to start by describing the **Participative or democratic** *style first. As Steve Jobs famously said, "It doesn't make sense to hire smart people and tell them what to do; we hire smart people so they can tell us what to do."[33] This style involves the leader including one or more employees in the decision-making process (determining what to do and how to do it). However, the leader maintains the final decision-making authority. Using this style is not a sign of weakness; rather, it is a sign of strength that your employees will respect.* **"As we look ahead into the next century, leaders will be those who empower others"** *...Bill Gates.*

The ***delegating style*** *is normally used when you have trained, highly skilled, and dependable employees whom you have diligently empowered to make limited decisions on specified tasks. Note that a leader is not expected to know everything—this is why you employ knowledgeable and skillful employees. Using this style is of mutual benefit—it allows them to become part of the team and helps you to make better decisions. This gives employees a sense of pride and a feeling that they are valuable contributors to the success of the organization.*

"The function of leadership is to produce more leaders, not more followers."[34]—Ralph Nadar.

In this style, the leader allows the employees to make the decisions. However, the leader is still responsible for the decisions that are made. This approach is used when employees can analyze the situation and determine what needs to be done and how to do it. You cannot do everything! You must set priorities and delegate certain tasks.

"The final test of a leader is that he leaves behind in others the conviction and will to carry on."[35]—Walter Lippman.

The Bible spells it out plainly in the book of Numbers 11:17: "I will come down and speak with you there, and I will take some of the power of the Spirit that is on you and put it on them. They will share the burden of the people with you so that you will not have to carry it alone. "[36]

The ***Authoritative or autocratic style*** *is the least of my favorites since it promotes a condescending, top-down management style and has no merit in Effective Leadership.*

The old traditional top-down management culture is being dismantled. However, I continue to experience the remnants of this type of culture being practiced. This is due to the lack of training and openness to the change that unfolds real tangible results. Dismantling the autocratic style not only improves a workplace culture but, at the same time improves the financial bottom-line results exponentially. This has changed the role of a manager from one who drives results and motivation from the outside into one who is a servant-leader—who seeks to draw out, inspire, and develop the best and highest work ethic within people from the inside out.

Chapter 7

How do You Measure Up? Is <u>Continuous Improvement</u> the Yardstick of Your Success As A Business Leader?

[29] *"For to everyone who has, more will be given, and he will have an abundance. But from the one who has not, even what he has will be taken away."[37] – Matthew 25:29*

One of the profound stories and anecdotes I have heard and read was the one about a very young, newly ordained priest who was strolling in the garden while pondering on some issues that seemed to bother him. An older priest noticed him and approached to ask him if everything was all right. The young priest replied that he was troubled by several questions regarding his Christian faith.

He also went on to say he felt that he was betraying his love for Jesus. He then looked up at the older priest and asked the question that was on his mind; "Am I a faithful priest, Father?" The older priest thought for a while and then replied, "Anyone who questions his own faith is truly faithful indeed."

Another reason I often challenge the status quo is the much-increased focus on cultural myths that have been spreading among our youth in our society over the last few decades. Namely:

1. *Yes, we can! We hear the words spoken aloud that we are the masters of our own destiny. We are told that you can be anything you want to be. True, we have many opportunities in the free world, but we all have personal limitations. Namely, we all cannot become a King & president just because we want to.*

2. *You can be the best in the world: Again, to be your best is very different from being the best. In North America, we throw around the word "awesome" so freely and recklessly that we are sometimes given false hope.*

3. *Everyone's a winner (everyone deserves a trophy): Clearly, all people are not winners when competing. Some lose. In addition to not being true, all those sentiments focus on success, not the value of being faithful.*

In Christian circles, success can easily become an idol. Tim Keller, in his book Counterfeit Gods, states:

"More than other idols, personal success and achievement lead to a sense that we ourselves are God, that our security and value rest in our own wisdom, strength, and performance. To be the very best at what you do, to be at the top of the heap, means no one is like you. You are supreme."[38]

For some, it is merely being in a successful geographical location. It reminds me of the lyrics of a Frank Sinatra song: "New York, New York."

"I want to wake up in a city.

That never sleeps

And find I'm king of the hill.

Top of the heap."

Thank God for those who recognized the importance of writing and copying down Scripture passages that give us a strong antidote to our cultures' misguided ideas of success.

Not all of us are endowed with equal skills, abilities, and opportunities.

I heard a story about an elderly Chinese woman who had two large pots, each hung on the ends of a pole, which she carried across her neck. One of the pots had a crack in it, while the other *pot was perfect and always delivered a full portion of water. At the end of the long walks from the stream to the house, the cracked pot arrived only half full.*

For two full years, this continued daily, with the woman bringing home only one and a half pots of water.

Of course, the perfect pot was proud of its accomplishments. But the poor cracked pot was ashamed of its own imperfection and miserable that it could only do half of what it had been made to do. After two years of what it perceived to be bitter failure, it spoke to the woman one day by the stream.

"I am ashamed of myself because this crack in my side causes water to leak out all the way back to your house." The old woman smiled and asked, "Did you notice that there are flowers on your side of the path but not on the other pot's side?"

"That's because I have always known about your flaws, so I planted flower seeds on your side of the path, and every day while we walk back, you water them." For two years, I have been able to pick these beautiful flowers to decorate the table. Without you being just the way you are, there would not be this beauty to grace the house."

Each of us has our own unique flaw. But it's the cracks and flaws we each have that make our lives together so very interesting and rewarding.

You've just got to take each person for what they are and look for the good in them.

So, to all the cracked pots that I love, have a great day, and remember to smell the flowers on your side of the path!

One passage that explains the intrinsic worth of each of us as individuals so beautifully is in Jesus' Parable of the Talents, as recorded in Matthew 25: 14-30.[39]A parable is a story Jesus told that had a spiritual lesson in it.

A workplace leader in a profit-driven secular environment is constantly looking for answers to his many questions. Therefore, we are thankful to know that the Bible has something profound to say about this topic. Through this parable, Jesus teaches that the Kingdom of Heaven is like a man going on a journey. Before he goes, he gives three workers different amounts of money, denominated by talents, which were weights used for money on that day. The actual value of a talent is not clear, but it was a very substantial amount of money to be entrusted to workers of that day.

To one, he gave five talents; to the second, he gave two talents. And to the third, he gave one talent; each was given talents according to their ability. Upon his return, he inquired about what they had done with the money. The first and second workers invested their talents, doubled their money, and received the master's praise. The third servant, who was given one talent, safeguarded his money but did nothing to increase it. As a result, the master condemned him for his inactivity. The parable of the Talent teaches us a few important lessons about the biblical meaning of success while dispelling the cultural myths listed above.

The narrative explains that each man was given talents "according to his own ability." The master understood that the one-talent servant was not capable of producing as much as the five-talent servant. Initially, we may read that and feel" that was inequitable, partial, and biased."

Each of us is made in God's image with abilities that are unique to our individual selves. The difference between "being the best" and "being the best you can be" lies in the focus and the measure of success. Being the best means outperforming everyone else in a particular field, sport, job, or activity. It's about achieving the highest rank or status among all competitors. The focus is on external comparison. Success is determined by how one's performance stacks up against others. This mindset often comes with immense pressure to constantly win or be at the top, as success is measured by being better than everyone else. Imagine an athlete who competes in a marathon with the goal of coming in first place. Their success is measured by finishing ahead of all other runners, regardless of their own personal best time.

My older sibling, while still in his early teens, emerged as a successful sportsperson, embodying a combination of physical prowess, mental resilience, and strong character. Physically, he possessed exceptional athletic skills, such as speed, strength, agility, and endurance, which were refined through rigorous training and dedication. Mentally, he consistently strived for improvement, excelling every year and winning several accolades, even at inter-province sports competitions. This was his God-given talent. However, at home, there was much parental pressure to excel in academics, and unfortunately, he fell short of my father's expectations of him in this respect. Historically, in many societies, education has been one of the few reliable means of social mobility. In societies where opportunities for professional advancement are limited, parents may push their children to excel in studies to ensure they have the best chances of success in a competitive environment. Our family was no different. Parental Expectations of academic success are often equated with future success in life, which reflects well on the family's social status. There is a strong societal expectation that children should excel in school, leading to pressure on parents and children alike. The desire of many parents for their children to excel in academics can be attributed to a combination of cultural values, historical factors, and practical considerations.

When parents fail to recognize the talents and strengths of their children, it can have several consequences. I witnessed my brother lose precious opportunities to reach his highest potential. It broke my heart to see him develop low self-esteem, doubt his abilities, and develop a lack of confidence in his skills.

Without encouragement or recognition, children might not develop or fully utilize their talents. They may abandon pursuits where they could excel. A lack of recognition can lead to emotional distance between parents and children. Children may feel misunderstood, unsupported, or unappreciated. Parents may push children into activities or paths that don't align with their strengths, causing frustration and resentment. Over time, the lack of acknowledgment can contribute to feelings of depression or anxiety, especially if the child feels their identity is being overlooked. Recognition from parents plays a key role in helping children understand who they are and what they are good at. Without this, children might struggle with their sense of identity. Encouragement, open communication, and a willingness to explore and nurture a child's unique talents are crucial for their overall development and well-being.

On the other hand, being the best, you can be means striving to reach your personal potential, regardless of how others perform. It's about self-improvement and personal growth. The focus here is on internal comparison. Success is defined by achieving your own goals and making progress based on your capabilities and effort. This approach is often more fulfilling, as it allows for personal satisfaction and growth without the constant need for external validation. Students work hard and often manage to significantly increase their test scores compared to their past performance. Even if they aren't the top student in the class, they've succeeded in being the best they can be by reaching their personal goal. For each of us, the result of the design that shapes our lives as an individual is not easily visible while each thread is woven together. It is only known to the mind of the Grand Weaver, so all we need is to be like clay in the safe and dexterous hands of the Potter.

"In a free society, absent of dishonesty and cronyism, disparity of wages is not a sign of injustice; it is the result of God's diversity within His creation. But even though we are not created equal regarding the talents given, there is equality found in this parable and in God's economy; it comes from the fact that it takes just as much work for the five-talent servant to produce five more talents as it does for the two-talent servant to produce two more talents. That is why the reward given to each by the master is the same. The master measures success by the degree of effort."[40]

However, this does not mean that "winning" or being the Best is wrong—if God has given you the ability to win when competing with others, and you give God credit. For example, Eric Liddell portrayed this in the classic movie, "Chariots of Fire." He said that "When I run, I feel (God's) pleasure." And he also stated, "To give that up would be to hold (God) in contempt. To win is to honor Him."[41]

God always gives each of us abilities and talents to accomplish His purpose.

"I can do all things through Christ who strengthens me" (Philippians 4:13).[42] In the parable, the Master expected his servants to do the best they could with what was entrusted to them. God expects us to generate a return by using our skills and abilities toward a productive end. The servant who received five talents had everything necessary to double his investment. The servant who received two talents had everything necessary to do the same. The servant who received one talent had everything necessary to produce one more, but out of fear, he chose to do nothing. More importantly, in God's economy, he lost an opportunity.

Genesis 1:28 says:

"And God blessed them. And God said to them, "Be fruitful and multiply and fill the earth and subdue it and have dominion over the fish of the sea and over the birds of the heavens and over every living thing that moves on the earth."

Nancy Pearcey, in her book Total Truth, explains why it's been called the "cultural" mandate. "The first phrase, 'be fruitful and multiply,' means to develop the social world: build families, churches, schools, cities, governments, and laws. The second *phrase, 'subdue the earth,' means to harness the natural world: plant crops, build bridges, design computers, and compose music. This passage is sometimes called the Cultural Mandate because it tells us that our original purpose was to create cultures and build civilizations—nothing less."[43]*

Tim Butler, from St. Ignatius Catholic community, Jesuit church of Baltimore, tells us:

- *"We are here as ambassadors of the Creator.*

- *We are created beings, placed into God's created world.*

We work at the pleasure of our Lord, and our work is to be driven by our love of our master."[44]

Real success in Christian life is not defined by worldly achievements, wealth, or status but by living in accordance with God's will and purpose. It involves cultivating a deep, personal relationship with God through faith in Jesus Christ and allowing that relationship to guide every aspect of one's life. Trusting and resting assured that all things work for the good of those who place their trust in Him.

Many speakers speak about "Positive thinking." Thinking positively is another way of saying, "Remain Hopeful." Isn't it wonderful to know that all of mankind need not simply hope against hope, but we can place our hopes in the hands of someone who has walked the talk? Someone who trod the path of pain, anguish, and suffering. Someone who became a part of human pain and suffering and who died and conquered death so that we can, experience a transformative relationship that offers eternal life, inner peace, guidance, strength, joy, hope, love, and purpose here and now. Continuously improving our leadership skills means growing in faith; it means aligning one's actions, decisions, and desires with God's commandments and teachings. Success is seen in living a life that honors God and reflects His love and grace. This may involve using one's gifts and talents to serve the church, spread the Gospel, and make a positive impact in the world. Ultimately, real success in Christian life is about glorifying God and building His Kingdom rather than seeking personal gain. It is about living in such a way that, at the end of one's life, one can hear the words, "Well done, good and faithful servant" (Matthew 25:21).

I learned that the human nature of Jesus is inextricably linked to his divine personality. In fact, leadership ability comes from his divine nature and not the other way around. I am now convinced that the true Christian worldview may have contrarieties but none of its message is ever contradictory.

Chapter 8

Disciplining Employees and How to Understand Difficult Working Relationships.

Correcting others in the right way is important for all. Many passages in Biblical scripture speak to this principle, as illustrated by the following examples: "And let us consider one another in order to stir up love and good works, not forsaking the assembling of ourselves together, as is the manner of some **but exhorting one another, and so much, the more as you see the Day approaching"** **(Hebrews 10:24-25). "And we urge you, brethren, to recognize those who labor among you, and are over you in the Lord and admonish you, and to esteem them very highly in love for their**

work's sake. Be at peace among yourselves. Now we exhort you, brethren, warn those who are unruly, comfort the fainthearted, uphold the weak, be patient with all" (1 Thessalonians 5:13-14). "But avoid foolish and ignorant disputes, knowing that they generate strife. And a servant of the Lord must not quarrel but be gentle to all, able to teach, patient, in humility correcting those who are in opposition, if God perhaps will grant them repentance, so that they may know the truth, and that they may come to their senses and escape the snare of the devil, having been taken captive by him to do his will" (2 Timothy 2:23-26).

How can Christian leaders approach correcting others in the right way? Leadership is the act of influencing and serving others out of Christ's interests but doing so with love, patience, and a gentle spirit in order to accomplish God's purposes for and through them. Understanding and showing empathy means you need to temporarily place yourself in their shoes to understand their needs, concerns, strengths, and weaknesses. Every employee is hired because they show their ability, attitude, and desire to embrace change during the hiring process as well as through the probation period.

Having done our best to teach and train an employee, it is important to hold them responsible and accountable to their job description as well as their work ethic. As workplace leaders, we must all suffer from one of two pains: discipline or regret. The role of emotional intelligence in leadership emphasizes empathy, self-awareness, and relationship management. Jesus says, "But to those of you who will listen, I say: Love your enemies, do good to those who hate you, bless those who curse you, pray for those who mistreat you."[45]

I have experienced that a workplace feels right when your relationships with everyone around you are cordial, pleasant, and peaceful as well. When this happens, the most difficult tasks seem doable; the most challenging projects come alive with clarity and purpose. If only we could let it sink deep into our hearts and comprehend with our minds that our lives at work are NEVER about work but always about the people and the kind of relationships we have built and nurtured over time.

Relationships are generally easy to nurture most of the time when you get along with those you meet, but most, if not all of us, at some time or another, have encountered difficulties getting along with some people. This could be true whether these people are at home, among your acquaintances or colleagues at work. It seems that the more we try to befriend such people, the more we tend to antagonize them and grow distant. Part of life is accepting that not everyone will like you.

If you really want to understand some very difficult people, then have kids and wait until they reach their teens. One may hold titles like Plant Manager, General Manager, CEO, director, or vice president, but the best title is what I have observed in the lives of my wife, my daughter-in-law, and my daughter as well. It is 'Teacher, Mother and Spouse.' When I look back at life as if in the rearview mirror, I can see how naturally mothers are leaders without even trying so hard. "Mothers endure labor and sleepless nights, and yes, this may top the list for many of us when we think of tough motherhood experiences, it's the emotional challenges that I've found to be the hardest. After all, when you love someone as deeply as you love a child, you become vulnerable in a way you never imagined possible. "[46]God feels this too unimaginably so, for we are made in His image.

*Reem Kassis, a former business consultant turned mama, writer, and cookbook author, describes her experiences with her daughter that resonate with mothers in general. Reem talks about her **not being able to take away her daughter's pain.** "When she had her first blood test, her first vaccine, and her first fever, when she fell and bumped her head; when she caught her finger in a drawer; and every other time she has cried because she was in pain, I would have given everything I owned to go through that pain instead of her. 'But I know I can't, and that breaks my heart into a million little pieces,' she concludes. "[47]*

Furthermore, a parent worries constantly as we realize we are not perfect human beings and we lack so much, far more than we can express. At the end of the day, we hope our best is good enough. A parent lives with uncertainty, hoping we have trusted God enough so that one day we can aim well and let go. A dear uncle from Smiths Falls, Ontario, who is now with the Lord, once said the wisest words to me: "Your kids are gifted to you, but they belong to God. They are like arrows in a quiver, so trust God, aim well, and let go." These words are now etched in my mind. We see wisdom in these words even more clearly now than we did at first. The realization that even a mother cannot control every outcome for her child could be the hardest, but it also leaves her with a sense of joy and connection that is unrivaled by anything else. That is why, in a heartbeat, she would do it all over again.

A mother's love for her child is as unconditional as it can get among all Homo sapiens. Did this happen overnight? Absolutely not. I am convinced that it is love that draws us even closer as a family than ever before. Our son and daughter, who are young adults holding important jobs, still find time in their busy schedules to call, talk, and spend time with us.

In the light of being a parent, how does it compare to being a Christian leader in the workplace? It is generally true that we do not have any emotional attachment to the people whom we work with. This emotional detachment ought to make it a tad bit easier to be professionally able to develop a good working relationship within the workplace. Nevertheless, the common element to success is surrendering the relationship to the omniscient God while encountering each situation with a keen sense that your decision must always be unbiased and without prejudice.

How can we love people at work when we don't even like them? Some of them do not like us, and worse, some of them hate and despise us. How can we even begin to nurture good working relationships with difficult colleagues and bosses? An employee in your workplace may not always be the kindest or nicest individual, but your genuine concern can bring out the best in people by being a good listener and always being respectful to others. You cannot control what others may say or do, but you can certainly control your own actions and words.

*As a leader and teacher, educating oneself and imparting education to others is your passport to the future, for tomorrow belongs to those who prepare for it today. You soon realize that as a teacher, you are an awakener. At times, you need to awaken yourself by embracing new ideas and problem-solving approaches. The art of **teaching** is the art of assisting discovery.*

*In the Gospel of Luke, the parable goes as follows: He told them this parable. "Which of you men, if you had **one** hundred **sheep** and **lost one** of them, wouldn't **leave the ninety-nine** in the* *wilderness and go after the **one** that was **lost** until he found it? When he has found it, he carries it on his shoulders, rejoicing.* "[48]

Each morning, when I wake up to the smell of freshly brewed coffee, it reminds me of the mission statement of STARBUCKS, a company that is performance-driven through the lens of humanity! "To inspire and nurture the human spirit—one person, one cup, and one neighborhood at a time.

OUR VALUES

Creating a culture of warmth and belonging where everyone is welcome. Acting with courage, challenging the status quo, and finding new ways to grow our company and each other. Being present is connected with transparency, dignity, and respect. Delivering our very best in all we do, holding ourselves accountable for results."[49] Again, in yet more difficult situations in building good, effective working relationships, scripture shows us a practical path to adopt in the Gospel of Luke.

Luke 6:27-28 Amplified Bible (AMP)

"But I say to you who hear [Me and pay attention to My words]: <u>Love</u> [that is, unselfishly seek the best or higher good for] your enemies, [make it a practice to] <u>do good</u> to those who hate you, <u>bless</u> and show kindness to those who curse you, <u>pray</u> for those who mistreat you.

The answer is that we cannot love them or make them like us right away because we are trying to reach the goal without working towards it. However, if we use the very words of Christ, taking the form of the rungs of a ladder, to help us reach upwards and onwards, then you create an effective ladder—a ladder of reconciliation.

"*Rung 4. LOVE*

Rung 3. DO GOOD

Rung 2. BLESS

Rung1. PRAY

Lesson learned: **It is better to lose an argument and win a relationship than to win an argument and lose a relationship.**

Chapter 9

Ethical Leadership

"Leadership is a combination of strategy and character. If you must be without one, be without the strategy."[50]—Gen. H. Norman Schwarzkopf.

According to the Collins Dictionary online, "if you have integrity, you are honest and firm in your moral principles." Personal integrity is an inborn moral conviction to do what is right and reject what is wrong, regardless of the consequences that are attached to one's decisions.

Why is Integrity Important?

Integrity in the workplace is so important as these traits provide your team with confidence, knowing that you are not only approachable but also highly dependable. As an immigrant to Canada, my first job was at an automotive parts manufacturing company, and the person I reported to always took notes while making his daily rounds. Joe realized that in a highly busy environment, it was quite easy to forget things unintentionally, and this provided him with a sure way of accomplishing all the tasks that were required of him. This not only helped him respond to each task over the course of the day, but it also gave his team the comfort of knowing that he took their requests seriously. Integrity is not just important on a personal level; it is also vitally important at a workplace level. Where there is open communication, good decision-making, and a strong moral compass guiding all decisions and actions, you will undoubtedly foster mutual trust. Whereas irresponsible behavior and distrust can create an uncomfortable and tense work environment. External customers, much like employees (internal customers) in your team, want to work with people who stand behind their mission statements and do what they say and say what they do. Who would want to deal with an organization that does not keep its word, that says one thing but does something else, or that offers bad products or services? They would not. Customers would not want to deal with an organization that is indifferent and cannot be trusted to follow through with what they have agreed upon. By being known for your integrity, you will gain trust and respect from the people around you. Management at all levels within the organization who are known for their integrity help their organizations to perform better.

"Integrity comes in many forms, but the most important traits that are expected at the workplace are dependability, honesty, loyalty, and good judgment."[51]

However, I have noted that Integrity can manifest in various forms, including:

Moral Integrity: Upholding ethical principles and doing what is right even when no one is watching.

Intellectual Integrity: Maintaining honesty in academic and intellectual pursuits, avoiding plagiarism, and acknowledging sources.

Professional Integrity: Adhering to professional codes of conduct and standards in one's work and interactions.

Personal Integrity: Being true to oneself, living in alignment with one's values and beliefs.

Interpersonal Integrity: Ensuring honesty, trustworthiness, and consistency in relationships with others.

Financial Integrity: Handling money and resources responsibly, avoiding fraud or dishonesty in financial dealings.

Emotional Integrity: Being authentic and genuine in expressing emotions and feelings. Overall, integrity encompasses honesty, sincerity, and consistency in thoughts, actions, and relationships.

Demonstrating integrity in the workplace involves various actions and behaviors. Here are some ways to do so:

Honesty and Transparency: Be truthful in your communications and interactions with colleagues, clients, and stakeholders. Avoid exaggerations, misrepresentations, or withholding important information.

Consistency: Remain consistent with your values and principles, even when faced with difficult situations or pressure to compromise.

Accountability: Take responsibility for your actions and decisions. Acknowledge mistakes, learn from them, and take steps to rectify any harm caused.

Respect: Treat everyone with respect, regardless of their position or background. Listen actively, consider others' perspectives, and avoid making derogatory or discriminatory remarks.

Confidentiality: Respect the confidentiality of sensitive information and data entrusted to you. Avoid gossiping or sharing confidential information inappropriately.

Fairness and Equity: Treat people fairly and impartially, ensuring equal opportunities and fair treatment for all. Avoid favoritism or discrimination based on personal biases.

Adherence to Policies and Regulations: Strictly follow company policies, procedures, and legal regulations. Avoid cutting corners or engaging in unethical behavior to achieve short-term gains.

Ethical Decision Making: Consider the ethical implications of your decisions and actions. Choose courses of action that align with ethical standards and principles, even if they are not the easiest or most convenient.

Supporting Others: Stand up for what is right and support colleagues who exhibit integrity. Encourage open dialogue and provide support to those who raise concerns about unethical behavior. By consistently demonstrating these behaviors, you can establish yourself as a person of integrity in the workplace and contribute to fostering a culture of trust, respect, and ethical conduct.

Admit to and learn from your mistakes— *Jesus asks why we are so skillful to see a speck in a brother's eye and so unable to* *notice the log in our own eye[52]. It seems human beings can recognize the smallest of sinful infractions in the lives of others while walking around with obvious and ugly sins of their own. Leaders are human beings who, like everyone else, are imperfect. This realization ought to encourage a leader to be open to learning, and in the process of learning, there is no shame in admitting to your misconceptions, incorrect presuppositions, or mistakes. "Make it your goal to be a person of integrity always, no matter how many temptations or challenges you face." [53]*

***Doctrine of clean hands** - Keeping things clean in relationships at a workplace involves maintaining professionalism, respect, and clear communication with colleagues. It involves avoiding gossip, conflicts, or negativity that can create tension or disrupt teamwork. It also means being accountable for your actions, treating others with kindness and fairness, and fostering a positive and inclusive work culture. Essentially, it's about promoting a healthy and harmonious atmosphere where everyone feels valued and supported.*

The above are great tips for demonstrating good ethical behavior; however, I was amazed to find an even better way. I learned that actually implementing these good tips into practice took a lot of time and effort. This was exhausting, as I frequently found myself referring to the tips to see if I was doing well. I wished my good ethical behavior could be expressed more easily and naturally.

*My daily Bible reading brought me to Paul's writing about the fruit of the Spirit found in **Galatians 5: 22-23. In the New International Version of the Bible, these verses read: But the fruit of the Spirit is love, joy, peace, forbearance, kindness, goodness, faithfulness, gentleness and self-control. Against such things, there is no law. <u>Galatians 5:22-23</u> as a <u>fruit of the Spirit</u> is self-control. The fruit of the Spirit is the change in our character that comes about because of the Holy Spirit's works within us. We do not become Christians on our own, and we cannot grow on our own. <u>Philippians 2:13</u> says, "It is God who is at work in you, both to will and to work for His good pleasure." Every good thing we do is the fruit of the Spirit's work in our lives.***

I learned that knowledge is good and can come from books, but the bible teaches that true motivation and desire to do the right thing come from within us.

Self-control ("temperance" in the KJV) is, of course, the ability to control oneself. This involves moderation, constraint, and the ability to say "no" to our baser desires and fleshly inclinations.

One of the proofs of God's working in our lives is our ability to control our own thoughts, words, and actions. This does not mean we are naturally weak-willed. As human beings, we are prone to

93

challenge the status quo, and sometimes we break the rules. The Bible calls it being a "slave to sin" (Romans 6:6). One definition of sin is "filling a legitimate need through illegitimate means."

I look at sin as acting and living independently of God. In the parable of the Prodigal son, as mentioned in the gospel of Luke 15:11-32, "There was a man who had two sons; and the younger of them said to his father, 'Father, give me the share of property that falls to me.' And he divided his living between them. Not many days later, the younger son gathered all he had and took his journey into a far country, and there he squandered his property in loose living". The sin committed by the prodigal son was not when he was in the act of loose living, but loose living was the consequence of turning his back on his father.

Is 53:6 says, "All we like sheep have gone astray; we have turned everyone to his own way; and the LORD has laid on him the iniquity of us all."

Without the power of the Holy Spirit, we are incapable of knowing and choosing how best to meet our needs. Even if we knew what would be best, such as not smoking, another need——such as comfort, would take precedence and enslave us again.

When we are saved by Christ's sacrifice, we are free (Galatians 6:1). That liberty includes, among other things, freedom from sin. "Our old self was crucified with him so that the body of sin might be done away with, that we should no longer be slaves to sin" (Romans 6:6). Now, as the Spirit gives us self-control, we can refuse sin.

Believers need self-control because the outside world and internal forces still attack (Romans 7 21:25). Like a vulnerable city, we must have defenses. A wall around an ancient city was designed to repel enemies. Judges at the gates determined who should be allowed in and who should remain outside. Soldiers and gates enforced these decisions. In our lives, such defenses might include avoiding close relationships with sinners, meeting with other believers, and meditating on the life-giving word of God. We don't exhibit self-control if we continually dally with things that can enslave us.[54]

Self-control naturally leads to perseverance (2 Peter 1:6) as we value the long-term good instead of the instant gratification of the world. Self-control is a gift that frees us. It frees us to enjoy the benefits of a healthy body. It frees us to rest in the security of good stewardship. It frees us from a guilty conscience. Self-control restricts the indulgence of our foolish desires, and we find the liberty to love and live as we were meant to.

Humility & Empathy

Leaders must have it ingrained in them that every day, you learn something new. "Everyone is your teacher. At times, you learn to emulate others, and at other times not to."[55]

Effective leaders are always good students, always willing to learn, and believe that no man is your enemy; every man is your teacher. To be good students one must be humble before God and before others. They will be humble, not servile, self-possessed, and not selfish. They will not need to be applauded or praised. They will recognize that their abilities owned will be the gift of a gracious God and will not have come through human achievement or natural talents. Consequently, they will not need to promote themselves, to boast, to pose, to advertise their skills. Their humility will make them personally secure, not continually needing the affirmation of others.

***Philippians 2:3-11** - [Let] nothing [be done] through strife or vainglory; but in lowliness of mind let each esteem others better than themselves.*

Thomas à Kempis, in his book, "The Imitation of Christ,[56]" reminds us that the malice of man, even in a seemingly militant workplace, cannot harm a good leader who maintains a clear conscience and shows the strength of humility. Such a man is always willing to acknowledge his own faults, he easily placates those about him and readily appeases those who are angry with him. This humble man experiences peace during many vexations because his trust is in God, not in the world.

Empathy & Body language

The story of the woman caught in adultery is found in the Bible, in the Gospel of John, chapter 8, verses 3-11. It recounts an incident where a group of scribes and Pharisees brought a woman caught in adultery before Jesus, intending to trap him. They asked Jesus about whether she should be stoned, as the law of Moses commanded. However, Jesus responded by saying, "Let any one of you who is without sin be the first to throw a stone at her." This caused the accusers to leave one by one, realizing their own guilt. Jesus then told the woman that he did not condemn her and instructed her to go and sin no more. The story is often cited as an example of Jesus's compassion and forgiveness. However, in the actual text, as shown below and described in the 8th chapter of John verses 3-11, the finer aspects of the story are very interesting, as is illustrated in Jesus' body language: **"³And the scribes and Pharisees brought unto him a woman taken in adultery; and when they had set her in the midst,**

⁴ They say unto him, Master, this woman was taken in adultery, in the very act.

⁵ Now Moses in the law commanded us, that such should be stoned: but what sayest thou?

⁶ This they said, tempting him, that they might have to accuse him. <u>But Jesus stooped down and with his finger, wrote on the ground</u> as though he heard them not.

⁷ So when they continued asking him, he lifted up himself, and said unto them, He that is without sin among you, let him first cast a stone at her.

⁸ <u>And again he stooped down and wrote on the ground.</u>

⁹ And they who heard it, being convicted by their own conscience, went out one by one, beginning at the eldest, even unto the last: and Jesus was left alone, and the woman standing in the midst.

¹⁰ When Jesus had lifted up himself and saw none but the woman, he said unto her, Woman, where are those thine accusers? Hath no man condemned thee?

¹¹ She said, No man, Lord. And Jesus said unto her, Neither do I condemn thee: go, and sin no more."⁵⁷

In a local church I attended, a visiting Jesuit priest, Fr. Fernandes, explained that in the underlined texts in verses 6 and 8, He is aware she did wrong, but he is also careful not to come across as intimidating and domineering, so he avoids embarrassing her further by staring her down. So, he simply stoops down and writes something in the sand.

Furthermore, in verse 8, he allows the conscience of the accusers to convict their hypocritical righteous attitude. His genuine love for his people is so deep that even in the process of disciplining them, he is carefully protecting their dignity and self-respect, not just of the accused but also that of the accusers.

Similarly, in a secular workplace, too, we can adopt Christian principles and empathy. To gain acceptance and followership, leaders need to have good social skills. They will like, even love others, and will be liked, even loved by others. Leaders who are reclusive and distant may bear some of the marks of leadership but will never really understand or empathize with their people. They will need to identify with the hopes, joys, pain, and ordinary issues that are important to their people. Leaders who constantly seek to be the center of attention are not, therefore, good leaders. However, good and effective leaders must love and serve their people.

Jesus wept over the city of Jerusalem (Luke 13:34). When his friend Lazarus was declared dead, the Scriptures tell us that this strong leader, Jesus, wept for His friend (John 11:35). When the sister of Lazarus was under pressure from her activist sister, Martha, Jesus came to her defense (Luke 10:42). Leadership without compassion is arid and sterile. Jesus, a strong, bold leader, revealed a sensitivity and compassion that enhanced and balanced His strength of character and dynamic leadership. Cultivate a heart that genuinely cares for those you are responsible for, even if they are not the most pleasant people to be around.

I remember an incident in a Toronto workplace. Howie, a certain Union steward, was always at loggerheads with the Supervisory staff, and very often his ire was felt by me and others at the corporate office. It seemed to me that no matter how much effort was put into making him feel we cared, it still was not enough.

Then, one day, I received the tragic news that his son had had an accident and unfortunately succumbed to his injuries. My heart genuinely felt grief for this person and his family, and so I made it a point to attend the funeral service, where I knelt in the corner of the funeral parlor and prayed for the family. After having paid my respects, I left silently all the time, praying while I drove home. It was not soon after this that I began to notice a remarkable change in his behavior towards the staff and myself. Later, I learned that I was the only management representative who attended.

Galatians 5:14: "For the entire law is fulfilled in keeping this one command: "Love your neighbor as yourself."

When your thoughts and actions genuinely emerge from your heart and not from a superficial desire to be noticed, then you will see strained relationships become more elastic and flexible. Only a supernatural God can truly change the hearts of humankind.

Chapter 10

Negotiating With Labor Unions and Non-Union Employees In An Ethical Way

If you are a manager or supervisor where the employees are represented by a union, it is not unusual that you will be required to prepare for an upcoming event that deals with a renewal of the existing Collecting Bargaining Agreement (CBA). This is by no means a small task, and preparing well for this crucial event is half the "battle" won. Having presided over and participated in ambitious, aggressive, and sometimes fierce meetings, I have learned one key lesson: "You reap what you sow" during the tenure of the contract.

The New Testament letter to the Ephesians 4:29 states, "Do not let any unwholesome talk come out of your mouths, but only what is helpful for building others up according to their needs, that it may benefit those who listen." Proverbs 10:19 says, "Sin is not ended by multiplying words, but the prudent hold their tongues."

PRACTICE THE DOCTRINE OF CLEAN HANDS WITHIN A UNIONIZED OR NON-UNIONIZED PLACE OF WORK:

A policy/union grievance is a complaint by the Union that an action, failure, or refusal to act by the employer is a violation of the Collective Agreement that could affect all members who are covered by the Collective Agreement. The goal is to receive a low number of grievances over a fixed time frame, which can be impossible in reality, especially when the number of employees is many, and depending on how militant the bargaining unit may be. John was a shift supervisor who worked in the organization for several years. Supervisors in this organization were considered Management staff and were hence not represented or covered by the Collective bargaining agreement. During this period, I observed that John maintained what seemed, at the time, a good relationship with employees who were represented by a very well-known union. While on the other hand, there were several other supervisors who were not, as indicated by the number of grievances they received within the same time frame. This seemed odd to me, so when I began to tally the number of grievances received, I found that John had received no grievances over the period of 12 months, while the other supervisors received a few grievances over the same time period.

Over several weeks of analysis, it became clear, and evidence showed that John had been making selfish deals with the employees during the tenure of the contract, which involved some of the following behaviors:

Favoritism: Giving promotions, raises, or opportunities based on personal relationships rather than merit. Allocating resources or projects to benefit themselves or their team at the expense of others and engaging in business deals or partnerships that benefited him personally but were not in the best interest of the company or its stakeholders–a clear conflict of interest.

It is critical to note that relationships with all employees must be dealt with in a fair and consistent manner and should never be manipulative for any reason. Some of these negative behaviors must be avoided, as noted below:

Withholding information: Keeping important information from employees or other stakeholders to maintain power or control over a situation.

Exploitative behavior and ignoring feedback: Taking credit for the work of others, disregarding employee well-being, or engaging in unethical practices to further personal interests. It is easy to disregard feedback or concerns from employees or stakeholders when making decisions that primarily serve the manager's own agenda. These examples highlight situations where managers prioritize their own interests over the well-being of their team, the organization, or other stakeholders.

Prioritize fairness and consider the needs and perspectives of all parties involved. *Prioritizing fairness in the workplace is crucial for maintaining a positive and productive environment. Here are some tips to help achieve that:*

Establish clear and transparent policies: Ensure that all employees understand the company's policies on hiring, promotions, compensation, and disciplinary actions. Transparency builds trust and reduces the likelihood of unfair treatment. Provide equal opportunities: Offer equal opportunities for career advancement, training, and development to all employees, regardless of their background, gender, ethnicity, or any other characteristic. Encourage diversity and inclusion in all aspects of the organization.

Implement fair hiring practices: During recruitment and selection, use objective criteria and standardized processes to minimize bias and ensure that all candidates are evaluated fairly based on their skills, qualifications, and experience. Address and prevent discrimination: Take proactive measures to prevent discrimination and harassment in the workplace. Provide diversity, equity, and inclusion training to employees and managers, and have clear procedures in place for reporting and addressing complaints.

Foster open communication: Promote open dialogue and feedback between employees and management. Create channels for employees to raise concerns or grievances without fear of retaliation and take prompt action to address any arising issues.

Lead by example: Demonstrate fairness and integrity in your own actions as a leader. Treat all employees with respect and fairness and hold yourself and others accountable for upholding the company's values and standards of conduct.

Regularly evaluate and adjust policies: Continuously monitor and evaluate your organization's policies and practices to identify any potential areas of bias or inequity. Be willing to adjust as needed to ensure fairness and inclusivity for all employees. By prioritizing fairness in the workplace, you can create a more inclusive and supportive environment where all employees feel valued and empowered to succeed.

Communicate openly and seek win-win solutions. *The following points can help to emphasize and cultivate this trait:*

Foster a culture of trust: Create an environment where employees feel safe and are encouraged to share their thoughts, ideas, and concerns without fear of retribution.

Practice active listening: Listen attentively to others without interrupting, show empathy, and seek to understand their perspectives before responding. Share information openly and honestly, especially when it affects employees or the organization as a whole.

Respect diverse points of view and encourage feedback: Encourage open and transparent communication in your interactions with others, including admitting mistakes and addressing concerns openly. Solicit feedback from employees at all levels and demonstrate a willingness to act on it and create forums, such as team meetings, where employees can freely express their thoughts and ideas. Maintain an open-door policy and make yourself available for discussions and feedback. Value and respect the diverse perspectives and opinions of others, even if they differ from your own.

Address conflicts constructively: Encourage open dialogue to resolve conflicts or disagreements in a respectful and productive manner. Do not let preconceived and presupposed notions interfere with your dialogue and ability while resolving conflicts. Even after resolving a conflict, it is important to ensure that communication is ongoing by following up on discussions, providing updates, and seeking clarification when needed. By practicing these principles, you can promote a culture of open communication that fosters collaboration, innovation, and trust in the workplace.

The Bible encourages us to "Refrain from exploiting your team members and others for personal gain." New International Version Leviticus 25:17 says, "Do not take advantage of each other but fear your God. I am the LORD your God."[58]

Seek the wisdom to understand, not undermine each individual member.

The book of Proverbs 2:6-9 For the Lord gives wisdom; from his mouth comes knowledge and understanding; he stores up sound wisdom for the upright. Understanding each individual in the workplace is essential for fostering positive relationships, collaboration, and a supportive environment. Here are some tips to help you achieve this:

Listen actively: Take the time to listen attentively to your colleagues and try to understand their perspectives, experiences, and concerns. Pay attention to both verbal and nonverbal cues to gain insight into their thoughts and feelings.

Show empathy: Put yourself in your colleagues' shoes and try to understand their emotions and experiences. Show empathy *and compassion towards their challenges and difficulties and offer support when needed.*

Ask questions: Don't hesitate to ask questions to learn more about your colleagues' backgrounds, interests, and preferences. Showing genuine curiosity about their lives and experiences can help you build rapport and deepen your understanding of them as individuals.

Respect diversity: Recognize and appreciate the diversity of backgrounds, perspectives, and experiences among your colleagues. Be respectful of differences and avoid making assumptions based on stereotypes or biases.

Observe and learn: Pay attention to how your colleagues interact with others, their communication styles, and their preferred ways of working. Observing their behaviors and preferences can help you adapt your approach to better communicate and collaborate with them.

Build trust: Establishing trust is key to understanding individuals in the workplace. Be reliable, honest, and transparent in your interactions, and honor your commitments to build trust and credibility with your colleagues.

Be approachable: Create an open and welcoming atmosphere where your colleagues feel comfortable approaching you with questions, concerns, or ideas. Foster open communication and be receptive to feedback from others.

Find common ground: Look for common interests or goals that you share with your colleagues and use them as a basis for building connections. Finding common ground can help bridge differences and strengthen your relationships with others.

Respect boundaries: Be mindful of personal boundaries and avoid prying or intrusive questions. Respect your colleagues' privacy and only engage in discussions or interactions that they are comfortable with.

Stay curious and flexible: Remain open-minded and adaptable in your approach to understanding individuals in the workplace. People are complex and multidimensional, so be prepared to continuously learn and adjust your understanding as you get to know them better. By following these tips, you can cultivate a deeper understanding of your colleagues as individuals, creating a more inclusive and harmonious workplace environment.

Proverbs 6:16-19

New Revised Standard Version Updated Edition

[16] *"There are six things that the LORD hates, seven that are an abomination to him:*

¹⁷ haughty eyes, a lying tongue, and hands that shed innocent blood,

¹⁸ a heart that devises wicked plans, feet that hurry to run to evil,

¹⁹ a lying witness who testifies falsely, and one who sows discord in a family. "⁵⁹

Be seen as a person of honor and integrity in all situations. *Being a person of honor in the workplace is essential for building a positive reputation and fostering professional relationships. Here are some tips to help you achieve that:*

Be reliable: Always fulfill your commitments and meet deadlines. If you agree to complete a task or project, make sure you deliver it on time and to the best of your ability.

Communicate effectively: Keep your supervisors and colleagues informed about your progress, any challenges you encounter, and any assistance you may need. Clear and timely communication is key to building trust and avoiding misunderstandings.

Respect others: Treat everyone in the workplace with courtesy and respect, regardless of their position or level of authority. Show appreciation for your colleagues' contributions and remain receptive to feedback and constructive criticism.

Maintain confidentiality: Respect the confidentiality of sensitive information you may have access to during your internship. Avoid discussing confidential matters with unauthorized individuals and handle sensitive data with care.

Demonstrate integrity: Act with honesty and integrity in all your interactions and decision-making. Avoid engaging in unethical behavior or cutting corners to achieve your goals. Upholding high ethical standards will earn you the respect and trust of your colleagues.

Take initiative: Look for opportunities to contribute and add value to your team or organization. Volunteer for tasks, share ideas, and offer to help your colleagues whenever possible. Proactively seeking ways to contribute shows your commitment and dedication. Be open to receiving feedback from your supervisors and colleagues and use it as an opportunity for growth and development. Take constructive criticism gracefully and use it to improve your skills and performance.

Stay professional: Maintain a professional demeanor at all times, in both your behavior and appearance. Dress appropriately for the workplace and avoid engaging in gossip or office politics. Focus on your work and strive to make a positive impression. By embodying these qualities and behaviors, you can establish yourself as a person of honor in the workplace, making a positive impact during your internship.

The Bible teaches us that we must be honest about the oath we take and uphold our oath so that we will be seen as a trustworthy and dependable leader.

Joshua 9:15 NIV: "Then Joshua made a treaty of peace with them to let them live, and the leaders of the assembly ratified it by oath."

PREPARING FOR BARGAINING

The union's bargaining team is usually selected through a process outlined in the union's constitution and by-laws; meanwhile, the employer designates the management team. Each team analyzes the current collective bargaining agreement to identify areas for improvement. Ideally, the local will reach out to other stakeholders to seek input on issues for potential proposals.

CONDUCTING NEGOTIATIONS

Negotiations typically involve several rounds of bargaining. Both the union and management sides express the rationale behind their proposals. Some contract provisions remain predominantly the same from contract to contract, while others, such as salaries, are bargained with each new contract. The parties may modify some sections, and either side may propose a new bargaining topic.

State law and court cases determine the mandatory, permissive, and prohibited subjects of bargaining.

RATIFYING THE CONTRACT

When the union and employer teams reach a tentative contract agreement, they review the proposed contract with their respective constituency groups.

The union holds a ratification meeting where employees can ask questions and offer opinions on the tentative contract agreement. Subsequently, individuals are then asked to vote on the tentative agreement, usually by secret ballot. A majority of votes determine whether the contract is ratified (accepted) or rejected.

The management team generally seeks approval from the governing body. If both sides ratify the tentative agreement, then the parties have a new (or successor) collective bargaining agreement. If the tentative contract agreement is rejected—by either party—the teams usually return to the bargaining table and continue negotiating until they reach a new tentative agreement for a vote.

RESOLVING A CONTRACT DISPUTE.

If the parties cannot reach an agreement, state laws generally specify the methods for resolving the dispute. Usually, the parties may use mediation, arbitration, and/or a strike or lockout to reach an agreement.

Negotiating with a labor union in an ethical way involves several key principles: The key to resolving all labor disputes is the proper understanding of the Collective Bargaining Contract. We see a good example of this in the book of Hebrews.

Hebrews 6:16 says," For men verily swear by the greater: and an oath for confirmation is to them an end of all strife."

Honesty and Transparency: Communicate openly and honestly with the union representatives about the organization's goals, constraints, and priorities. Avoid making false promises or misleading statements.

Respect for Collective Bargaining Rights: Recognize and respect the union's right to represent its members' interests and engage in collective bargaining. Avoid attempts to undermine or circumvent the bargaining process.

Fairness and Equity: Ensure that negotiations are conducted in a fair and equitable manner, with both parties given the opportunity to present their interests and concerns. Avoid tactics that seek to exploit power imbalances or unfairly disadvantage the other party. Approach negotiations with a sincere intention of reaching a mutually acceptable agreement. Engage in meaningful dialogue, listen to the other party's perspectives, and work collaboratively to find common ground. We explicitly learn from the Biblical New Testament book of Colossians that we must not seek to be judgmental in discussions with our fellow employees and Trade union representatives.

The Bible emphasizes this again in the book of Colossians 3: [9] "Do not lie to one another, seeing that you have put off the old nature with its practices [10] and have put on the new nature, which is being renewed in knowledge after the image of its creator."

Compliance with Laws and Regulations: Adhere to all applicable labor laws, regulations, and contractual obligations governing the negotiation process. Avoid engaging in any unlawful or unethical conduct, such as coercion, intimidation, or discrimination.

Respect for Workers' Rights: Recognize and uphold workers' rights to fair wages, benefits, working conditions, and representation. Ensure that all proposed changes or agreements prioritize the well-being and interests of the workers.

Conflict Resolution: Handle disputes or disagreements that may arise during negotiations in a constructive and respectful manner. Aim to resolve conflicts through dialogue, mediation, or other peaceful means rather than resorting to confrontation or hostility. By adhering to these ethical principles, organizations can foster a collaborative and respectful relationship with labor unions, promote trust and goodwill among workers, and ultimately achieve fair and sustainable labor agreements.

Collective bargaining is a process in which unions and employers discuss and exchange ideas. Offers are made for demands, and the involved parties concerned try to agree, disagree, or find a compromise in order to reach a written agreement.

Most times, bargaining occurs when an existing contract is going to expire. But sometimes, a local will be negotiating a first contract after organizing a new bargaining unit. Both sides form bargaining teams and gather information.

The resulting approved contract legally binds both parties. Each round of successor negotiations allows the parties to revisit existing agreements. It is crucial to keep the promises that are made to your employees and Trade Union representatives. If you do not, then you can expect to encounter reprisals, and this will cast a shadow of doubt on your character.

Ezekiel 17:18 states, "Because he despised the oath and broke the covenant because he gave his hand and yet did all these things, he shall not escape."

Chapter 11

Vision, Strategy, and Understanding the Christian Dilemma

I heard it said that there is a proven strategy to walk out of any casino with a small fortune, and it works 100% of the time: All you must do is walk into the casino with a large fortune.

"If you do not know where you are going, every road will get you nowhere."[60]— Henry Kissinger.

<u>*Vision*</u>

Incorporating Christian values into workplace diplomacy involves treating colleagues with respect, practicing honesty and integrity, showing empathy, and seeking reconciliation in conflicts. It's about fostering an environment of understanding, forgiveness, and grace while also maintaining professionalism and productivity.

Jesus left his disciples with the commission to spread the good news throughout the world. In this commission, Jesus presented his chosen disciples with a vision (what they would achieve) and a strategy (how they should achieve the vision). **In the gospel of Mark 6:7-11**

[7]Calling the Twelve to him, he began to send them out two by two and gave them authority over impure spirits.

[8] These were his instructions: "Take nothing for the journey except a staff—no bread, no bag, no money in your belts.

[9] Wear sandals but not an extra shirt.

[10] Whenever you enter a house, stay there until you leave that town.

[11] And if any place will not welcome you or listen to you, leave that place and shake the dust off your feet as a testimony against them."

We also see Jesus choosing strategies throughout his ministry, such as choosing ordinary people to be his disciples and standing outside the established church.

Christian stability refers to the steadfastness and resilience grounded in Christian faith. It involves relying on God's guidance and strength during times of uncertainty or difficulty maintaining a sense of peace and trust amidst challenges. It's about fostering an environment of understanding, forgiveness, and grace while also maintaining professionalism and productivity.

Thinking on your feet – Disaster on Highway 401

It was the early hours of the morning, and I was on my way to work. Just as I did every morning, I took the usual exit on Highway 401. It usually takes me approximately 45 minutes from home to my place of work. I love my morning drive because it gives me time to sip my coffee and listen to my favorite country songs. It was not unusual for the majority of the drivers on this highway to drive a tad over the allowable limit. This route is typically favored by truckers carrying heavy loads heading towards the Canada – USA border. Today was no different. Just in front of me was a pickup truck with barn-style doors. All of a sudden, one of the barn doors swung open, and I noticed a tall, large dog, like a Great Dane, inside. The dog gradually moved toward the edge of the moving truck, and a song came on the radio station. It was Carrie Underwood singing one of my favorites: 'Jesus, Take the Wheel.' To my horror, the dog decided to step off the moving vehicle landed in the center of the lane and rolled over a few times. There was just enough distance between me and the dog to allow me to instantly react by turning my emergency vehicle flashing lights on, controlling the speed of the truck behind me, as I brought my car to a safe halt on the extreme lane. I then jumped out of my car and frantically waved for all the vehicles to slow down and stop. Every car and truck across all four lanes came to a safe halt. The dog was in a daze but standing tall and still. With the help of another kind-hearted gentleman, we managed to move him to the back seat of my van. We successfully managed to track the humane society and the owner, and fortunately, the story ended happily. A few weeks later, the Ontario Humane Society, along with the dog's owner, invited me to their annual meeting and presented me with a humanitarian award as a sign of gratitude. That was a kind gesture, but in my heart, I knew that without God's grace and presence of mind, the outcome could have been tragic.

The lesson I learned from this incident is that good leaders must trust God when faced with making decisions. When people look to them for a decision, they must take time to review and pray about it first. Of course, there will be times when you are not left with the luxury of time in which you must make a decision, especially when it concerns health and safety. I had the opportunity to save the life of Memphis, the name of this big Great Dane. The only words I could recollect at the time, just moments before the incident, were,

"Whatsoever you do unto the least of my brethren, you do unto me," *says the Lord. It was humbling to be equated with an animal, but it also reminded me that, although I was made in His image, perhaps I have, at times, reacted to my baser instincts whenever I did not stop long enough to make better choices.*

Also, this incident taught me that God provides us with opportunities to stand up for those who cannot speak for themselves, and He trains us and molds us into the person He wants us to be. Effective leaders think of others and are not content to see injustice, suffering, or abuse. They will not only be appalled by injustice but will also do what they can to address it. They will not only be saddened when people fail to live in peace; they will also seek to be peacemakers. They will not only be uncomfortable when others struggle, and they do not, but will also do what they can to redress imbalances within society. Good leaders possess a social conscience.

When decisive action was needed, Jesus acted. When the Temple was despoiled by manipulative, unscrupulous commercial interests, Jesus overturned the money changers' tables (Matthew 21:12). When the howling wind and raging sea threatened to overturn the boat, Jesus cried out, "Peace be still" (Mark 4:39), and a great calm came upon the sea.

Of course, sometimes the decision will be to await events—to not take a decision! But nothing is more frustrating in a leader than an inability to conclude.

Trusting your team-mates

"Don't be afraid to take a big step when one is indicated. You can't cross a chasm in two small steps."—purportedly quoted by David Lloyd George.

Effective leaders are imbued with natural common sense. They just know how to behave, what to say and when to say it; following no set formula, they make mature and timely decisions. Much of leadership comes down to old-fashioned common sense. People possessed with common sense are generally easy to identify and commend themselves to others. The Scriptures tell us that all wisdom comes from above and those who are natural leaders, who have the gift of common sense, realize that this precious gift has indeed come from above. Place your trust in those whom you lead, and sooner or later, they will meet your expectations.

Building a robust team and empowering them to take ownership of their work is a crucial aspect of effective leadership. However, some leaders tend to micromanage their team by monitoring every email and interaction, even for trivial tasks such as getting a glass of water. This approach is counterproductive and does not benefit either the team or the manager. No one can build and sustain a great company if there is no trust. Therefore, it makes no sense to recruit the best people only to tie their hands by not giving them the freedom to perform. Great leaders understand that the soul of their business is their team, and they must trust their team to produce their very best work. After all, that's why you recruited them in the first place. So, if you want to be a leader, give your team the space to work, and create an environment free from the impediments of toxicity, then you will witness significant growth in your company and, more importantly, in your team.

I heard someone at work say that high trust results in lower costs, and low trust results in higher costs of operation. If you are doing the right things for the right reasons—the honest desire to help others—it pays great dividends.

MORAL DILEMMA: WHERE IS GOD WHEN I AM FACED WITH PROBLEMS BEYOND MY CONTROL?

Frank was a newcomer to our altruistic support group in Kuwait. He had already attended a few sessions so far. He was invited to participate in one of the workshops that I was assigned to lead. Each workshop was divided into sub-groups of five to six participants. As the discussion progressed, I noticed that Frank seemed unusually quiet and seemed lost in thought. When he was asked to share his thoughts, he hesitated. To me, he seemed like a determined young man, his eyes reflecting a mix of anxiety and hope.

After a long pause, he told us he needed a job, and every day, he poured over job listings, his fingers worn from sending countless applications. The weight of his desperation was evident in his restless demeanor as he eagerly awaited responses that rarely came.

After the session, I asked if he had a few moments to talk, and we walked over to a coffee shop. He explained to me how he felt driven by the need to secure his future. He tirelessly pursued every lead, willing to take on any role that would provide him with a sense of stability and purpose. However, his mother worked as a caregiver for a wealthy family, and under the law, this meant he was also considered an employee of the same wealthy family. He was repeatedly denied a work permit, which left him feeling profoundly frustrated and helpless. Each rejection deepened his despair, leading him to question his worth and future prospects. The constant setbacks began to erode his confidence, leaving him feeling trapped and powerless as his dreams and plans remained just out of reach. The emotional toll of repeated denials also led to alienation and disenchantment with the system, fueling a sense of injustice and hopelessness.

I told him that I did not have any answers for him, but I knew someone who might. I asked him if he was open to saying a prayer with me. He said he had never said a prayer before and did not know how to. I encouraged him to talk to God, explaining that prayer was simply a conversation with God. Several weeks passed before I saw Frank again.

His employer gave him a task to clean up his massive villa, which he diligently completed. He explained how his conversation with God lasted for an hour and was not exactly pretty or respectful. Then, out of sheer exhaustion, he slept for three hours that afternoon. Upon waking, he related feeling a strange inner peace, a sense of calm and tranquility. Even though his situation was the same, he felt a new strength and a sense of fulfillment and gratitude for life as it was. Then, he noticed his employer's car approaching in the distance. After he had satisfactorily checked his work, just out of the blue, his employer handed him his release letter. This one document would enable him to secure a job and become independent. In his heart, he knew the power of prayer and how he was now convinced that it helped him connect with a higher power, fostering a sense of spiritual closeness and purpose.

The account of Peter walking on water is found in the Bible in the book of Matthew, Chapter 14, Verses 22-33. Here is the passage: Matthew 14:22-33 (NIV) [22] Immediately, Jesus made the disciples get into the boat and go on ahead of Him to the other side while He dismissed the crowd.

23 After He had dismissed them, He went up to a mountainside by Himself to pray. Later that night, He was there alone.

24 The boat was already a considerable distance from land, buffeted by the waves because the wind was against it.

25 Shortly before dawn, Jesus went out to them, walking on the lake.

26 When the disciples saw Him walking on the lake, they were terrified. "It's a ghost," they said and cried out in fear.

27 But Jesus immediately said to them: "Take courage! It is I. Don't be afraid."

28 "Lord, if it's you," Peter replied, "tell me to come to you on the water."

29 "Come," He said. Then Peter got down out of the boat, walked on the water and came toward Jesus.

30 But when he saw the wind, he was afraid and, beginning to sink, cried out, "Lord, save me!"

31 Immediately, Jesus reached out His hand and caught him. "You of little faith," He said, "why did you doubt?"

32 And when they climbed into the boat, the wind died down.

[33] *Then those who were in the boat worshiped Him, saying,
"Truly you are the Son of God."*

*Lesson learned: Work diligently in your present situation;
do everything you humanly can, then let go and let GOD help you
do the impossible.*

*It was passed around, perhaps as a "tongue-in-cheek"
comment during the threat of COVID-19, that the World Health
Organization announced that dogs cannot contract COVID-19.
Hence, dogs previously held in quarantine can now be released. To
be clear, WHO let the dogs out? Also, who knew that the comment
"I wouldn't touch them with a six-foot pole" would become a
national policy, but here we are! Supply and demand issues caught
us unawares. The price of commodities started to rise at a rate not
in step with our budget. Fear and apprehension that things could
get worse caused many to stock up on items for the proverbial
"rainy day." News of Job layoffs became part of the conversation
around the water fountain and cafeteria. The jobs of so many people
were on shaky ground. Until now you felt secure, and your recent
appraisal was proof of it. Suddenly, you feel like "Simon of Cyrene"
caught up in the passion.*

*In today's world, we are not just dealing and coping with the
healthcare protocols and preventative measures, but we are also
asking deep questions about our Faith, God, and the meaning of life.*

If God exists, then why is there so much fear, pain, and suffering in this world? Don't look at me… I don't have all the answers, but I can tell you what I do have: I have evidence that is logical, empirically verifiable, and experientially relevant. This evidence supports my belief that God is in control, but NOT without my permission. Once we surrender our lives to HIM, only then can we find that coping mechanism and the ability to go through the problems we face and emerge even stronger than before.

When we reach that point in life where, through no fault of our own, we suddenly find ourselves on the horns of a dilemma: bills must be paid; Lenders of mortgages and loans offer very little compassion and leeway. For some, it is a struggle even to put food on the table. The question of where God fits in all this looms overwhelmingly large and threatens our faith.

HOW DOES A CHRISTIAN RESPOND WHEN WRONGFULLY OR UNJUSTLY DISMISSED AT YOUR WORKPLACE:

In situations like wrongful dismissal from work, the Christian way involves responding with grace, forgiveness, and seeking reconciliation if possible. This may include praying for guidance, forgiving those who wronged you, and approaching the situation with humility and integrity. It's also important to seek justice through appropriate channels, such as legal recourse, if necessary, while still maintaining a spirit of love and compassion towards others involved.

Sometimes, it is also important to evaluate the culture that exists in your current workplace. "I've seen employees' self-worth shattered because they were repeatedly mistreated in the workplace. In that case, finding a company that values you and does not tolerate a hostile environment is critical. That means taking those toxic relationships off the table, distancing yourself, and moving on."[61] Don't be afraid to burn your bridges. The reflection of who you are in your own mirror must never be distorted by the dark silhouettes in the background.

In recent times, a variety of factors have impacted our economy. These include increasing inflationary costs, lack of raw materials, logistics problems, geopolitical reasons, interest rates, and housing crisis. Despite these challenges, we have witnessed many individuals and several organizations, including major retail outlets, that served Canadians and built a great team in Canada. However, through no fault of the vast number of employees, they had to make the tough decision to wind down operations in Canada. Over the last few years prior we saw hundreds of jobs lost when these giant organizations shut down their Canadian operations. Anxious employees were glad to find new opportunities, though many were not so fortunate. The stories don't end here. Several familiar businesses, both retail and manufacturing, continue to face

similar challenges. The one looming question being asked is, why??
But I ask, why not? Why not expect to see more of this heartbreaking
news when politicians and dictators cannot be stopped from
dismantling and disrupting our economy for their own personal
greed for money, power, and land?

There is still hope for humanity in the face of tyrants and so-
called "leaders" of various countries, who threaten its extinction
vis a vis nuclear weapons. All it takes is for a few wise men to be
empowered and wear the whole armor of God, which God provides.
The armor has a belt of truth, a breastplate of righteousness, shoes
of peace, a shield of faith, a helmet of salvation, and a sword of the
Spirit. The belt of truth refers to believing the revealed truth of God's
word. Without it, we cannot stand. We need to recognize and elect
such Godly men to come together and decide to place their real and
strong moral convictions ahead of geo-political reasons. This will
help our world's elected leaders send a strong message that bullies
will not be allowed to succeed in their nefarious activities. It will
also send an even stronger message to our new generation that in
this 21st century, countries must invest most of their GDP (Gross
domestic product) in education and health care, NOT in amassing
arms and ammunition. Thinking human beings must ACT now to put
an end to this war; alas, otherwise, war will end all of humanity.

The Greek philosopher Epicurus rejected the idea of an
omnipotent and omnibenevolent God (as summarized by David

Hume): "If God is unable to prevent evil, then he is not all-powerful. If God is not willing to prevent evil, then he is not all good."

Where do I begin? I have learned that none of what is happening should be beyond our understanding. There is, after all, a logical explanation for God's position in all of this. I am prompted to hum the tune of the song by Julie Andrews in the movie Sound of Music: "Let's start at the very beginning, a very good place to start." The very first book of the Bible puts everything in perspective.

In Genesis 1, we read:

God blessed Adam & Eve and said unto them, **"Be fruitful, and multiply, and replenish the earth, and subdue it: and have dominion over the fish of the sea, and over the fowl of the air, and over every living thing that moveth upon the earth.** [29] **And God said, Behold, I have given you every herb bearing seed, which is upon the face of all the earth, and every tree, in the which is the fruit of a tree yielding seed; to you, it shall be for meat."** *God recognized that it was all good! Then, something happened. Alas, the sin of disobedience caused a fracture in the relationship between God and mankind.*

The extent of the broken relationship between God and humankind is now described in **Genesis 3:16: "Unto the woman he said, I will greatly multiply thy sorrow and thy conception; in** *sorrow, thou shalt bring forth children: and thy desire shall be to thy husband, and he shall rule over thee. [17] And unto Adam, He said, because thou hast hearkened unto the voice of thy wife, and hast eaten of the tree, of which I commanded thee, saying, Thou shalt not eat of it: cursed is the ground for thy sake; in sorrow shalt thou eat of it all the days of thy life; [18] Thorns also and thistles shall it bring forth to thee; and thou shalt eat the herb of the field; [19] In the sweat of thy face shalt thou eat bread, till thou return unto the ground; for out of it wast thou taken for dust thou art, and unto dust shalt thou return."*

John Lennox, Professor of Mathematics at Oxford University, in one of his dialogues, states that pain, suffering, thorns, and thistles are the new inheritance, and yes, a fracture of basically two kinds: "Moral fracture through their disobedience and Natural fracture"[62] and separation from God, since Adam and Eve no longer could access the perfect ecological life that was intended for them and their descendants (all of us).

When things happen to us that are beyond our control, we are tempted to feel somehow it is our fault. There are people who may fuel this thought and jump to the conclusion that the setback is somehow a sign of God's punishment. Such a person can be seen as someone who is speaking from a moral high ground – and fear-mongering. This does not bring people closer to God, but in fact, it drives them further away. Believers become agnostic, and people who are agnostic can drift away to Atheism or unbelief in God altogether.

*How do I go about knowing what is grounded in philosophical thinking and what is not? Let us take a closer look at what Christianity has to say. And I found that in **Luke 13: 1-5** [1] **"At that very time, there were some present who told Jesus about the Galileans whose blood Pilate had mingled with their sacrifices.** [2] **He asked them, 'Do you think that because these Galileans suffered in this way, they were worse sinners than all other Galileans?'** [3] **No, I tell you, but unless you repent, you will all perish as they did.** [4] **Or those eighteen who were killed when the tower of Siloam fell on them—do you think that they were worse offenders than all the other people living in Jerusalem?** [5] **No, I tell you, but unless you repent, you will all perish just as they did."**[63]*

In the New Testament, we see overtones of similarity in HIS message - In JN 3:16 says, "God so loved the world...." Death and love are mentioned in the same sentence. Being humans with limited perception of anything outside of the 3D world we live in; we find it rather difficult that there can be anything beyond death. JN 3:16 is not simply talking about God's love but HIS unconditional love. In God's mind, death is the pathway into the originally intended life that was planned for you and me through his creation of Adam and

Eve. What bothers us most is not just the certainty of death, but the uncertainty of life.

"In a universe of electrons and selfish genes, blind physical forces and genetic replication, some people are going to get hurt, other people are going to get lucky, and you won't find any rhyme or reason in it, nor any justice. The universe that we observe precisely has the properties we should expect if there is, at the bottom, no design, no purpose, no evil, no good, nothing but pitiless indifference."[64]

If you are looking for a simple answer to the question of pain and suffering, then Richard Dawkins' explanation will suffice. I think the real answer is more complex than that. We want the truth, even if it may not be so simple.

Before we look at the different schools of thought on this matter, let's take a couple of minutes to evaluate the academic perspectives of the three most major disciplines. Science, Philosophy & Religion. Christianity is as rational as science. Many have been influenced by atheists' thinking, like Richard Dawkins, Christopher Hitchens, Sam Harris, and others, that Faith is a religious word and not based on any evidence. I want to tell you that Faith is an ordinary word and a belief system that is based on real evidence. Truth can be plausible when it undergoes tests of logical consistency, empirical verifiability, and experiential relevance.

Science and belief in God are not equal and opposite; in fact, science and God can co-exist in the most amazing sense. God, like theology, Arts, Music, and literature, are not natural sciences. However, the study of cosmology, the physical world we live in, and the laws that govern our planet are all-natural sciences.

C.S. Lewis said that men became scientific because they expected to see Law in nature, believing in a Lawgiver. This was true for Newton, Keppler, Galileo, and so many others, including our own modern-day co-mapper of the human genome, Dr. Francis Collins. In some small way I cannot help to reiterate that in my own field of Engineering, I spent all my working life in the application of scientific laws and principles. I then cannot help but admit that not one single law that governs the motion and reliability in the solid, dependable functioning of our planet was invented. They were all discovered, which means that they pre-existed in nature.

"The Christian God is not distant from us in our pain and struggles; in fact, he becomes part of it."[65] The only way one can understand another person's anguish and desperation is to put yourself in their shoes. This is exactly what Christ did for us when He took our shortcomings and nailed them to the cross along with Him so that we might find a way to run from death into the safety of His outstretched arms. God does not promise us freedom from our problems, but as long as you place your trust in Him, He is always there to help you find a way through them. In his letter to the church

in Corinth, a converted Paul, who was earlier a persecutor of early Christians, encourages us with his words in 1Cor 10:13: " No temptation has overtaken you except such as is common to man, but God is faithful, who will not allow you to be tempted beyond what you are able, but with the temptation will also make the way of escape, that you may be able to bear it. "[66]

Chapter 12

Wisdom In A Time of Crisis - The Christian Approach

It was a cool day in February, and the usual whirring sound of the machines on the shop floor was suddenly replaced by a loud and piercing scream from someone in trouble. An employee's finger got caught in a forming machine during the plastic extrusion process, leading to a sudden halt in operations. Colleagues rushed to help, while supervisors swiftly enacted safety protocols and called for medical assistance. While he was being loaded on a stretcher and into the ambulance, I looked at his finger and realized that one-half of his forefinger was severed. At the last second, I asked the ambulance to wait while I carefully retrieved the severed part of his *finger, which was still lying within the blades of the forming press. I placed it in an icepack and accompanied him to the hospital, all the while praying over the finger and asking God to work a miracle. The employee was in tears. Fortunately, the best surgeon was on duty that evening, and when he met us, I asked him if it was possible to reattach his severed finger. I recall his words even today. He said, "I will do my best. You just sit here and pray." A few days later, it became obvious that the operation was successful as blood began to flow through his finger once again as the wound was on its way through the healing process. Needless to say, this employee was deeply touched and grateful for the wisdom, presence of mind, and timely medical assistance.*

A good leader takes all necessary steps to deal with times of crisis because it's their responsibility to ensure the well-being and stability of their team, organization, or community. By taking decisive action, communicating effectively, and implementing strategies to address the crisis, a good leader can help mitigate its impact, maintain morale, and guide others through the challenges. Additionally, effective crisis management can help build trust, demonstrate leadership competence, and ultimately lead to a quicker recovery and stronger resilience in the face of future crises.

A story is told of a young man who was searching for the secret of wisdom and heard about a guru high in the Himalayas who knew. So, he set off to find the guru, going through much hardship and travail until finally, high in the mountains, he found the Master sitting in the lotus posture.

"Tell me, oh master!" he cried. "What is the secret of wisdom?"

The master replied, "Good judgment."

"But how do you get good judgment?" asked the young man.

The master replied, "Experience."

"And how do you get experience?" the young man persisted.

"Ah," said the Master. "Bad judgment".

Outside of the cross of Jesus Christ, there is no hope in this world. That cross and resurrection at the core of the Gospel is the only hope for humanity. Wherever you go, ask God for wisdom on how to get that Gospel in, even in the toughest situations of life.

*How many of you, after being shut in during COVID, went out cottaging, portaging, or simply on a picnic? My greatest wish is that **someday I will be able to wake up in the morning stress free.** I want my life to be peaceful and stable, that I would have a great job and I would be able to look over my balcony or porch and see a natural sight, free from commotion or traffic jams or horns blaring.*

IF YOU WERE GRANTED A WISH TODAY, WHAT WOULD IT BE?

Very often, even the great men in antiquity found themselves face to face with crises of one sort or the other.

As mentioned in Chapter 1 of this book, on his deathbed, David gives his son Solomon some last words of advice to ponder upon.

David dies, and Solomon is given the Kingdom. In 1 Kings 3, we are told that Solomon loved, walked, and worshiped God. This pleased God, and HE came to Solomon in a dream when he went to Gibeon to offer sacrifices and tell Solomon to ask for anything. What was Solomon's response:

- *He says in verse 6: Lord, you have shown great kindness to your servant David (**THANKING FOR THE PAST**) 1 Thessalonians 5:18 (in everything give thanks, for this is the will of God concerning you).*

- *I am only a little child (**HUMILITY**)*

- *The people are too many for me to handle (**Admits his fears—he is desperate and dependent on God's** favor)*

*God tells Solomon, in **1 KINGS 3:9,** that because he did not ask anything for himself alone, HE will also grant him long life and riches along with wisdom and a discerning heart.*

Solomon governed with great wisdom. The biblical narrative mentioned in 1 Kings 3:16–28 recounts that two mothers living in the same house, each the mother of an infant son, came to Solomon. One of the babies had been smothered to death, and each claimed the surviving boy, who was alive, as her own. Calling for a sword, Solomon declared his judgment: the baby would be cut in two, each woman to receive half. The mother who was willing to give the child to the other woman to save his life was the true mother. The false claimant agreed to have the child cut in half. Solomon understood that the true mother would rather give up the child than see it killed.

I heard of this humorous anecdote about a bus driver who found himself in a situation one morning where two women were squabbling over the last available empty seat. The conductor had already tried to intervene but to no avail. So, the driver shouted, "Let the ugly one take the seat!" As a result, both women stood for the rest of the journey. I couldn't help thinking that this anecdote certainly had a "Solomon's wisdom" ring to it.

DAVID & GOLIATH (1 Samuel 17) in verse 37: "The LORD who rescued me from the paw of the lion and the paw of the bear will rescue me from the hand of this Philistine." David used no armor or spear because he was comfortable being who he was: just a shepherd.

Furthermore, in verse 45, David said to the Philistine, "You come against me with sword and spear and javelin, but I come against you in the name of the LORD *Almighty, the God of the armies of Israel, whom you have defied. "*

David was desperate, but his trust was not in his prowess and ability to use his slingshot or his own skills; it was in the name of the Living God.

IS KNOWLEDGE WISDOM?

The Gospel of Matthew (22:36-37) reminds us that we ought to "Love God with all your heart, soul and MIND – we are supposed to use our minds. " While the world puts so much emphasis on doing things logically and intellectually, God chooses to resolve issues through HIS wisdom. Thinking logically involves the faculty of reasoning and objective understanding. Intelligence is the ability to acquire knowledge and skills, but wisdom is about more than just having knowledge as well as one's experience and common sense. It is said that Knowledge is knowing that bell peppers, hot peppers, and green peas are biologically considered fruit; **wisdom** *is not putting it in a bowl of fruit salad.*

Intellect is like the knives and motorized blenders in your kitchen, but intelligence is the wisdom to know when and how to use them. God's ways are as different from ours, as far apart as the heavens are from the earth.

In the Old Testament book called Judges 7:1-25 we read that there was Gideon, who faced the Midianites. He had an army of

32,000 men, and God instructed him to send many home till he was left with just 300. Why such unconventional methods?? We find the answer in Judges 7:2, "The people with you are too many for me to give Midian into their hands, lest Israel becomes boastful, saying, MY own power has delivered me." God works in such unique and seemingly ridiculous ways just so that we cannot claim that we did it ourselves. "He always chooses the weak things of this world to confound the mighty and the foolish things of this world to confound the wise." God does not do this because he wants to show that he is all-powerful, but instead, He wants us to understand that, as frail and sinful human beings, we will become so boastful, which in the end will cause us to fall deeper and deeper into pride. If there is any sin that God hates the most, it is the sin of pride. It was vanity and pride that caused the fall of Satan from grace. Just like a good shepherd, He wants us to stay near Him and not wander so far as to become unreachable from His ever-saving power and grace.

I wish to remind you of the words mentioned in the NT Gospel of Matthew 7:7: "Ask and it will be given to you; seek and you will find; knock and the door will be opened to you." At first glance, it appears that God is opening up His promises for us to ask just about anything, and He will provide it. Upon closely studying His words, we recognize that in HIS wisdom, HE built a hedge around this promise. We see this explained to us in James 4:2-4 – "² You desire but do not have, so you kill. You covet, but you cannot get what you want, so you quarrel and fight. You do not have it because you do not ask God. ³ When you ask, you do not receive, because you ask with wrong motives, that you may spend what you get on your pleasures."

Where do we get wisdom from?

James 1:5 tells us that "if anyone lacks wisdom, seek GOD." Also, the book of Proverbs 1:7 says, "The fear of the Lord is the beginning of wisdom." This is often misinterpreted to mean that one should be afraid of God. If God is Love, all forgiving and wants us to have a life of fullness, then it goes to show that the real meaning is that we should fear losing the relationship we have with God. It certainly does not mean that God is a policeman waiting to strike us down every time we sin. We need to turn to Him in obedience and seek to carefully avoid the occasion of sin because sin alienates and draws us away from God.

Is 30:21 says that "when we turn to the right and to the left, we will hear a voice." This is the voice of our conscience which grows more sensitive as we listen and reflect on God's teachings. Joshua 1:8 urges us to meditate on HIS word night and day and to do what it asks for us to be successful and prosperous.

Here's a beautiful poem titled "A NEW LEAF" that says so much about how each new day is a gift from God to make a difference and to be different:

"He came to my desk with a quivering lip; the lesson was done.

"Have you a new sheet for me, dear teacher? I've spoiled this one."

I took his sheet, all soiled and blotted, and gave him a new one, all unspotted.

And into his tired heart, I cried, "Do better now, my child."

I went to the throne with a trembling heart; the day was done.

Have you a new day for me, dear Master? I've spoiled this one.

He took my day, all soiled and blotted, and gave me a new one, all unspotted. And into my tired heart, he cried, "Do better now, my child."[67]

When we have exhausted all our hoarded resources and our strength has failed us before the day is even half done, we too are drawn to the Master as we cry out: "Do you have another day for me, master? I have spoiled this one."

That's how God deals with us. We try to do something good with our lives, but it turns into a mess. We try to make the best decisions with good intentions, but things get messy, and the more we try to fix the mess, the worse it gets.

Then we reach the point where all we can do is just stand back and wonder how we got into the mess we're in, and we just stand there in tears because we can't think of anything else to do.

That's when God, who has been observing us all along, walks into our lives, picks us up, loves us, and forgives us, even though our mess gets all over Him.

*Right now, if you're in the midst of a mess and you don't know how to get out, before you go to the phone, go to the throne— the foot of the cross of Christ, in humility and in a spirit of contrition. Your concerns are not uncommon, and no matter what situation you find yourself in, remember that God does not play favorites. If you surrender every outcome to Him, He will give you the grace to accept it somehow. In the letter to the church of Corinth, Paul tells us in 1 Corinthians 10:13 that we may need to wrestle with the cares of this world, but we do so by God's power. We may need to see a temptation to its end, but God is faithful. When tempted to presume upon the grace of Christ, our Lord and Master, God will empower us to endure—for our good, the good of the church, and for His glory. Lessons from the lives of great leaders in antiquity repeatedly show us that men and women must avoid falling into the traps of our own making, namely, **Ego and Pride**. This leads to a **lack of humility and forgiveness,** which in turn leads to **an unteachable spirit.***

Lesson learned: The acronym for WISDOM is <u>Walk</u> <u>in</u> <u>step</u> to <u>discern</u> and <u>obey</u> our <u>master.</u>

Chapter 13

Accountability: How Leaders can Demonstrate Accountability through Their Actions, Decisions, and Behaviors, Setting a Positive Tone for the Rest of the Team

1. Definition and Importance:

Leadership accountability is the obligation and willingness to take responsibility for one's actions. When you lead a team, and errors occur while on your watch, you are also required to take responsibility for the outcomes of the project or endeavor, including the actions of your teammates. Now, this may seem unfair, as you might justify a bad outcome as not directly you're doing. It could be that a teammate went off on a tangent and contributed to the failure. Your righteous anger may goad or stimulate your natural inclination to lay blame where it lies. However, Scripture makes it clear that leaders are called to a higher standard of accountability. As leaders they are responsible to be an example . . . and so their failure is also to be an example. These are Paul's words on why you must fight The Good Fight of Faith, as the apostle Paul writes in his letter to Timothy where he says:

¹¹ "But as for you, man of God, shun all this; aim at righteousness, godliness, faith, love, steadfastness, gentleness. ¹² Fight the good fight of the faith; take hold of the eternal life to which you were called when you made the good confession in the presence of many witnesses. ¹³ In the presence of God who gives life to all things, and of Christ Jesus who in his testimony before Pontius Pilate made the good confession."⁶⁸ (1 Timothy 6:11-13).

<u>*LEADING BY EXAMPLE*</u>

Monica was the Sales Manager, a person with a good work ethic and a trustworthy employee. A verbal quote for a million dollar's worth of widgets to be used in an automotive plant was verbally accepted by a potential customer. The customer's visit to our manufacturing plant ended with much appreciation. We shook hands, and I was delighted. The following morning, I briefed

Monica on the deal and asked her to meet the customer in person in order to finalize the deal with a written and signed approval. A few hours later, I received a telephone call from Monica; she said she was calling from her car in the customer's parking lot and was literally sobbing. She admitted that she goofed up because she was in a hurry and misquoted the numbers as well as the delivery dates, which infuriated the customer. She returned to my office, clearly still embarrassed. The following manager's meeting with the team commenced as usual. I informed the team that the contract was in jeopardy and that we were trying to do our best to salvage it. She was so relieved not to be directly blamed, and after the meeting, she came to my office to thank me for having her back. She learned from this mistake and was eternally grateful for how I handled it. She went on to be one of the best Managers we had. By the way, we also managed to salvage the contract.

In a team setting, you must set an example of trust. Remember, this does not mean that if an employee is, in fact, responsible for a bad outcome, his or her actions should be ignored or go unpunished. Follow the golden rule: Praise in public; discipline in private.

In order to build a trustworthy, well-informed, and effective team you will be proud of, it is critical to keep the following advice in mind:

- *Setting Clear Expectations: Discuss the importance of clearly defining roles, responsibilities, and expectations for leaders within an organization.*

- *Transparency and Communication: Highlight the role of open and transparent communication in fostering accountability within a leadership framework.*

- *Accountability Structures: Discuss the implementation of systems and processes to hold leaders accountable for their actions and outcomes.*

- *Learning from Failure: Explore how leaders can take responsibility for mistakes and failures, using them as opportunities for growth and improvement.*

- *Recognizing and Rewarding Accountability: Discuss strategies for recognizing and rewarding leaders who consistently demonstrate accountability in their roles.*

- *Building a Culture of Accountability: Explore ways to cultivate a culture where accountability is valued and embedded throughout the organization.*

- *External Accountability: Consider how leaders can be held accountable not only internally but also externally to stakeholders, customers, and the broader community.*

- *Challenges and Pitfalls: Address common challenges and pitfalls in fostering accountability within leadership roles, along with strategies to overcome them. By addressing these topics, you can provide a comprehensive exploration of leadership accountability and its importance in organizational success.*

ACCOUNTABILITY MEANS FOLLOWING GUIDELINES

SOLOMON allowed his pride to dictate his actions: The biblical account, as stated in (1 Kings 10:26–29) is that Solomon accumulated 1,400 chariots and 12,000 horses, which he stationed in the chariot cities and also with him in Jerusalem. He also made silver and gold as common in Jerusalem as stones and cedar as abundant as sycamore in the foothills.

Solomon was extremely wealthy, perhaps viewed as the wealthiest king of his times, similar to modern figures like Jeff Bezos or Elon Musk, according to the Bloomberg Billionaires Index at the time of writing this text.

Solomon was required to follow some guidelines, as mentioned in Deuteronomy 17:14-20.

The summary of the guidelines given to Solomon was:

*"[14] **When** you enter the land that the LORD your God is giving you and have taken possession of it and settled in it, and you say, "Let us set a king over us like all the nations around us," [15] **you** are to appoint over yourselves the king whom the LORD your God shall choose. Appoint a king from among your brothers; you are not to set over yourselves a foreigner who is not one of your brothers.*

[16] But the king must not acquire many horses for himself or send the people back to Egypt to acquire more horses, for the LORD has said, 'You are never to go back that way again.' [17] He must not take many wives for himself, lest his heart go astray. He must not accumulate for himself large amounts of silver and gold.

[18] When he is seated on his royal throne, he must write for himself a copy of this instruction on a scroll in the presence of the Levitical priests. [19] It is to remain with him, and he is to read from it all the days of his life, so that he may learn to fear the LORD his God by carefully observing all the words of this instruction and these statutes. [20] Then his heart will not be exalted above his countrymen, and he will not turn aside from the commandment, to the right or to the left, in order that he and his sons may reign many years over his kingdom in Israel.

The root of Solomon's downfall was his marriage to many pagan women who "led his heart astray" from Yahweh, and he lost sight of the guidelines given to him. This was the very danger of which Israel was warned by Moses in Deuteronomy 7:1-4.

PRIDE GOES BEFORE A FALL

NEBUCHADNEZZAR (DANIEL 4 34-37) We have another example of a great King whose pride brought about his downfall.

Nebuchadnezzar II, a prominent Babylonian king, is often cited for his immense pride in the Bible, particularly in the Book of Daniel. His prideful nature is illustrated in Daniel 4, where he boasts about his achievements and the magnificence of Babylon, attributing all glory to himself rather than to God. This arrogance leads to a divine punishment: Nebuchadnezzar is driven from his kingdom and lives like an animal for seven years. This period of humiliation ends only when he acknowledges God's sovereignty. The story underscores the theme that pride goes before a fall and highlights the importance of humility before divine authority.

GOD UNDERSTANDS HUMAN SUFFERING, WHICH IS A CONSEQUENCE OF MAN'S SINFUL NATURE.

On the other hand, one must also understand that God does not promise us a problem-free life. Jesus understands human suffering and becomes part of it.

In the biblical narrative mentioned in the book of Job, we read in the following verses that, "In the land of Uz there lived a man whose name was Job. This man was blameless and upright; he feared God and shunned evil. ² *He had seven sons and three daughters,* ³ *and he owned seven thousand sheep, three thousand camels, five hundred yoke of oxen and five hundred donkeys, and had a large number of servants. He was the greatest man among all the people of the East.*

The Book of Job is a complex narrative in the Hebrew Bible that addresses the question of human suffering. It begins with Job, a righteous man, being subjected to immense suffering, including the loss of his wealth, children, and health. Despite his friends' attempts to explain his suffering as punishment for sin, Job maintains his innocence and questions God's justice. In the end, God appears to Job and asserts His sovereignty, emphasizing the limitations of human understanding. Job is then restored and blessed with even greater prosperity. The book explores themes of suffering, faith, and the mystery of divine providence.

[20] *Even though he suffered all these calamities, through no fault of his own, he did not blame God for his misfortunes. Instead, Job got up, tore his robe and shaved his head. Then he fell to the ground in worship* [21] *and said:*

"Naked, I came from my mother's womb, And naked, I will depart. The Lord gave, and the Lord has taken away; May the name of the Lord be praised."

[22] *In all this, Job did not sin by charging God with wrongdoing.*

One of the key truths to grasp from the Book of Job is that we must trust God even when we cannot understand Him, even when He is thoroughly confusing to us.

- *The central statement in the book is one of Job's closing comments to God: "I had heard reports about you, but now my eyes have seen you" (42:5).*

Hebrew Bible scholar John Walton puts it this way in his commentary on Job:

"God's answer to Job does not explain why righteous people suffer because the cosmos is not designed to prevent righteous people from suffering. Job questioned God's design, and God responded that Job had insufficient knowledge to do so. Job questioned God's justice, and God responded that Job needed to trust Him and that he should not arrogantly think that God can be domesticated to conform to Job's feeble perceptions of how the cosmos should run. God asks for trust, not understanding, and states the cosmos is founded on his wisdom, not His justice.

Human pain and suffering do not always occur as a clear consequence of anyone's sin. There may be a reason, but there may not be. God Himself said that Job's suffering was not warranted for "any reason." The answer to this story is that sometimes terrible things happen for no reason discernible to any human. The point is that God's world is very good, but it is not perfect or always safe. It has order and beauty, but it is also wild and sometimes dangerous, like the two fantastic creatures He avows. So, back to the big question of Job's or anyone's suffering: Why is there suffering in the world? Whether from earthquakes, wild animals, or from one another? God doesn't explain why. He says, "We live in an incredibly complex, amazing world that, at this stage at least, is not designed to prevent suffering."

That's God's response. Job challenged God's justice, and God responded that Job didn't have sufficient knowledge about our complex universe to make such a claim. Then Job demanded a full explanation from God, and what God asked Job for was trust in His wisdom and character. So, Job responds with humility and repentance. He apologizes for accusing God of injustice and acknowledges that he has overstepped his bounds.[69]

Chapter 14

What Is So Great About Jesus?

HISTORICAL evidence of Jesus and why this is such a stumbling block to many non-Christian worldviews.

The litmus test for ancient manuscripts often involves several criteria:

1. *Age and Authenticity:* Determining the age of the manuscript and its authenticity through scientific methods such as carbon dating and paleography.

2. *Textual Integrity:* Assessing the accuracy and consistency of the text across different copies or fragments of the manuscript.

3. Corroboration: Comparing the content of the manuscript with other historical sources or archaeological findings to verify its reliability.

4. Historical Context: Evaluating whether the content of the manuscript aligns with the historical context in which it was purportedly written.

5. Expert Analysis: Seeking insights from scholars and experts in relevant fields such as archaeology, linguistics, and textual criticism to validate the manuscript's authenticity and significance.

These criteria help researchers in determining the trustworthiness and value of ancient manuscripts for understanding historical events, cultures, and ideologies.

According to Catholic tradition, referencing the CCC (Catechism of the Catholic Church), it does not definitively state who the first writer of the New Testament was. It emphasizes that the gospels are the primary source for understanding the life and teachings of Jesus Christ. However, some Christian scholars suggest that the Gospel of Mark, written around AD 65-70, might have been the first Gospel written. Catholics believe that the Holy Spirit inspired the authors of all the New Testament books, which were written over several decades in the first century AD. The New Testament consists of various genres, including Gospels, letters (epistles), and apocalyptic literature, all of which are considered divinely inspired.

Other Christian scholars also believe that the Gospel of Mark was the first New Testament book written around AD 65-70. Yet there are several others who postulate the Q Source hypothesis that there was an earlier collection of Jesus' sayings, known as the "Q document," which both Matthew and Luke might have used in addition to Mark. However, this document is hypothetical and not extant. These debates continue to propagate as studies on the early writings of the New Testament are unraveled.

These differing views highlight the complexities of determining the exact chronology of the New Testament writings, which remains a topic of scholarly debate and interpretation.

– So, by that reckoning, there are writings about the life and death of Christ circulating from people who were eyewitnesses. This is the best sound argument for early dating.

Attested in writings reported by Tacitus is not the only non-Christian writer of the time who mentioned Jesus and early Christianity. The earliest known references to Christianity are found in 'Antiquities of the Jews,' a 20-volume work by the Jewish historian Titus Flavius Josephus, written around 93–94 AD, during the reign of emperor Domitian.[70]

Tacitus, the historian who was a heathen, wrote in the year A.D. 55, detailing passages about the crucifixion of Christ and his sufferings. The Jewish historian Josephus (37 - 100 CE) and Roman historian Tacitus (56 - 120 CE) are two figures commonly cited as the earliest extra-Biblical sources for a historical Jesus. Apparently, Josephus mentions Jesus twice in his work Antiquities of the Jews, which was written around 93-4 CE. That's about six decades after Jesus' lifetime. Also, Tacitus' mention of Jesus in the Annals, which was written around 116 CE, comes well over 80 years after Jesus' death.

1st generation: Matt, Mk, Lk John, Paul, and the others. 2nd generation: Patheus of Rome, Polycarp, Ignatius

The earliest teachings of the apostles (kerygma) were in the form of the creed: ^{1} Cor 15:3-7, dated within months of his death and resurrection. This kind of historical evidence is what makes historians drool. The early believers died for their beliefs, and this can be argued that many people die for their beliefs, BUT no one dies for a known lie.

"The disciples' willingness to suffer and die for their beliefs indicates that they certainly regarded those beliefs as true. The case is strong that they did not willfully lie about the appearances of the risen Jesus. Liars make poor martyrs.[71]"

Bart Ehrman, known as an agnostic atheist, has written numerous books challenging traditional views of the Bible himself. Even Ehrman surveys the arguments Christ mythicists have made against the existence of Jesus, an idea that was first mooted at the end of the 18th century. New Testament scholar Bart Ehrman, in his book, "Quest of the Historical Jesus of Nazareth,"[72] mentions the Historical Argument for Jesus of Nazareth. He not only attempts to prove the historical reality of a man called "Jesus of Nazareth," he also sharply criticizes scholars who have sought to develop a new paradigm in the study of Christian origins—scholars who have claimed that Jesus was a mythical, not historical, figure and that the traditional, Jesus-centered paradigm for studying the origins of Christianity must be replaced by an actual science of Christian origins. In the present volume, some of those scholars respond to Ehrman's treatment of their research and findings, showing how he has either ignored, misunderstood, or misrepresented their arguments. And the sources behind them, which scholars have discerned, still contain some accurate historical information. Ehrman notes that so many independent attestations of Jesus' existence are actually "astounding for an ancient figure of any kind."

Regarding Jesus' birth as described in the Old Testament book of Isaiah 7:14: "Therefore the Lord himself will give you a sign: The virgin will be with child and will give birth to a son and will call him Immanuel."

Isaiah 9:6: "For to us a child is born, to us a son is given, and the government will be on his shoulders. And he will be called Wonderful Counselor, Mighty God, Everlasting Father, Prince of Peace."

Micah 5:2: "But you, Bethlehem Ephrathah, though you are small among the clans of Judah, out of you will come for me one who will be ruler over Israel, whose origins are from old, from ancient times."

Psalm 22:16-18: "Dogs have surrounded me; a band of evil men has encircled me; they have pierced my hands and my feet. I can count all my bones; people stare and gloat over me. They divide my garments among them and cast lots for my clothing."

Isaiah 53:3-7 is especially unmistakable: "He was despised and rejected by men, a man of sorrows, and familiar with suffering. Like one from whom men hide their faces, he was despised, and we esteemed him not. Surely, he took up our infirmities and carried our sorrows, yet we considered him stricken by God, smitten by him, and afflicted. But he was pierced by our transgressions. He was crushed for our iniquities; the punishment that brought us peace was upon him, and by his wounds, we are healed. We all, like sheep, have gone astray; each of us has turned to his own way, and the LORD has

164

laid on him the iniquity of us all. He was oppressed and afflicted, yet he did not open his mouth; he was led like a lamb to the slaughter, and as a sheep, before her shearers were silent, so he did not open his mouth."

My search for the historical Jesus has convinced me that my faith is neither biased nor blind, but rather, it is based on rock-solid evidence.

In a humorous anecdote, I once heard when a little girl asked her father, "How did the human race start?" The father answered, "God made Adam and Eve; they had children, and so all mankind was made." Two days later, the girl asked her mother the same question. The mother answered: "Many years ago, there were monkeys from which the human race evolved." The confused girl returned to her father and said, "Dad, how is it possible that you told me the human race was created by God, and Mum said they developed from monkeys?" The father answered, "It is very simple. I told you about my side of the family, and your mother told you about hers." You may have heard this humorous anecdote several times in various forms. However, the message it carries is that almost everyone ponders the question of our origin and purpose in life.

When the sin of disobedience entered our world, God banished our first parents from their home, where they enjoyed a *perfect ecological and providential life in every way. They did not kill, steal, or commit adultery, so do you think that the punishment matched the crime? After all, it was just a little, teeny tiny sin of disobedience.*

The verdict was not based solely on the act of disobedience in itself but on the exponential power of making choices, good or bad; that was the real problem. SIN has a ripple effect. Over the millennia, the sensitivity toward making wrong choices has dulled, and the gravity of sin & depravity has exponentially increased.

Isn't it somewhat ironic that we, as individuals in a society, crave a safe haven where our kids can grow without fear or intimidation? How many of us here today are first-generation immigrants to this great land of Canada?

If you took the time to ask yourselves or your parents their primary reason, their answer invariably is "for a better life for our family"—the word "better" is a relative term—better than what? This answer varies depending on which part of the world you actually immigrated from.

We look for a good society, a just society, a society that accepts and loves you just the way you are, and finally, when and if you make mistakes along the way, you hope to be forgiven so that you can pick yourself up, dust off the dirt, and do better next time.

Parents want their children to live in a world devoid of evil and where JUSTICE, LOVE, & FORGIVENESS flourish.

In the gospel of Matthew, we are instructed to love God with all our heart, soul, & MIND—yes, even God expects us to use our minds.[73]

"So, when God, back in eternity, was faced with the greatest crisis of all—the entrance of SIN into HIS perfect universe—it is no wonder that HE did not meet it in the way we might expect. Here was a conflict involving the entire universe; God's character and credibility were in question. His creative genius and perfection were challenged. His beloved creation, created in His own image, was threatened. The spiritual world waited with bated breath, wondering how HE would respond. If God had wanted, He could have simply spoken Satan and his angels out of existence, just as He had spoken the universe into existence. But this would mean that He would be breaking His own purpose of creation. God created beings, both angelic and human, endowing them with the power to choose. If He violated that purpose, then His creation would end up being automatons. Love would cease to be a choice. God chose the way that He always chose, the way that we would assume was foolish. He decided that He would fight a rebellion with a cross. It was a strange plan, and many called it foolish...and still do.

Jesus arrived in our world in such a manner that He already had several strikes against him, preventing HIM from getting ahead. "[74]

Jesus seemed to violate all the rules of getting ahead. He was brought up in a simple carpenter's home, possibly without even a comfortable bed to sleep on. He never wrote a book, led an army, or was enrolled in any schools, yet at a pre-teen age, He held conversations that astonished and enlightened even the Doctors of Religion. Then, instead of choosing bright and brilliant doctors of the law as His followers, He went ahead and chose some uneducated fishermen as his torchbearers. "Always choosing the weak things of this world to confound the mighty and the foolish things of this world to confound the wise." [75]

Jesus could have easily led a revolt against Rome... with His ability to work miracles. He instead appeared to have no sense of timing. When it seemed that the people were ready to make Him King, He turned the crowds away and went into the garden to pray. The hopes of His followers reached a peak once more when he rode into Jerusalem, and the people waved palm branches amidst the shouts of praise...surely, He was about to assume power. But only days later, He allowed his enemies to lead him to a place called Golgotha, where He allowed them to nail His hands and His feet on a plain old rugged cross.

George E Vanderman expounds the crucifixion at a deeper level and understanding: Jesus' death was not one surrounded by family or with nurses. Nor like Stephen, who looks up and sees the savior standing over him with sympathy and love. Nor like any Christian who dies with at least the hope of rising again.

"The wages of sin is death and separation, and so the sinner MUST die without the hope of rising again, and so must Jesus...Even for a moment, fear gripped our LORD, and in His humanity, He may have felt, even for a fleeting moment, that the sins of the world would be so offensive to God the Father, that the separation would just be FINAL....it was at this time, HE exclaimed, 'Father, why have you forsaken me.'"

So fierce was the battle that Jesus was hardly aware of what was happening below the cross. His tormentors jeered scornfully, saying, "He saved others; now Himself He cannot save." This contest was decided in the shadow of death, not in the light of HIS father's presence. It was only in the final moments that HIS faith in his father broke through the darkness, and HE knew that HE had won."[76]

A poem by Studdert Kennedy:

"And sitting down, they watched him there, the soldiers did,

While they played their game of dice, Jesus made HIS sacrifice,

And died upon the cross to rid GOD'S world of sin.

He was a gambler too, my Christ, for He took His life and threw it away for a world to redeem,

And before His agony was done and crowned the day with a crimson crown, HE knew that He had won."[77]

What appeared to be a terrible mistake turned out to be the most brilliant move LOVE could ever make... No wonder then, before HE gave up His last breath, HE said the words: "It is Finished."

Have you heard about little six-year-old Daniel, who decided one Saturday morning to make his parents pancakes? He found a big bowl and spoon, pulled a chair up to the kitchen counter, opened the cupboard, pulled out the heavy flour can, and spilled it on the floor. He scooped some of the flour from the floor into the bowl with his hands, mixed in most of a cup of milk, and added some sugar, leaving a floury trail in his wake, which by now also had some tracks left by his cat. Daniel was covered with flour and was getting frustrated. He wanted this to be something very good for Mom and Dad, but it turned out very bad. He didn't know what to do next, whether to put it all into the oven or onto the stove. He also didn't know how the stove worked.

He saw his cat licking from the mixing bowl and reached to push her away, accidentally knocking the egg carton to the floor.

Frantically, he tried to clean up this monumental mess but slipped on the eggs, leaving his pajamas white and sticky. It was then that he saw his dad standing at the door. Big tears welled up in Daniel's eyes. All he had wanted was to do something good, but he had made a terrible mess. He was sure that a scolding was coming, maybe even a spanking. But his father just looked at him with a smile. Then, walking through the mess, he picked up his crying son, hugged him, and loved him, getting his own pajamas white and sticky in the process.

That's how God deals with us. We try to do something good with our lives, but it often turns into a mess. We try to make the best decisions with good intentions, but things get messy, and the more we try to fix the mess, the worse things get.

Then we get to the point where all we can do is just stand back and wonder how we got into the mess we're in, and we just stand there in tears because we can't think of anything else to do. That's when God, who has been observing us all along, walks into our lives, picks us up, loves us, and forgives us, even though our mess gets all over Him. Right now, if you find yourself in the midst of a messy situation, and you don't know how to get out, then take a bold step, even at the cost of feeling and sounding foolish, and surrender to Jesus, ask Him to come into your life and take over and show you the right way, His way. And remember, just because we mess up doesn't mean we must stop trying because sooner or later,

God will help us to get through, and He always gets it right. "When we were utterly helpless, Christ came at just the right time and died for us sinners (Romans 5:6-8). Even when we were still messy, God sent His son, Jesus Christ, to die for us. Now that we know Jesus and He has taken on our mess and cleaned us up, He will make sure to bring us into God's kingdom without spot or blemish. Yet, there are all kinds of questions that can pop up in our minds. Paul, the writer of the biblical letter to the church of Corinth, brings this up as well, wherein he says that if Christ has not been raised, our preaching is worthless, and so is our faith.[78] This should bring hope to many. However, it also raises questions about the complexity of the Godhead, just as in the Trinity.

The concept of the Trinity is considered blasphemy by some and is quite confusing to the monotheistic concept. Definition of TRINITY: God is ONE in being and THREE in persons. A being is that quality that defines you WHAT you are. A person is what makes you WHO you are.

The doctrine of the Trinity, which teaches that God is one in essence but three in persons (Father, Son, and Holy Spirit), is often misunderstood as a contradiction. However, the Catholic Church and other Christian traditions maintain that the Trinity is not a contradiction when properly understood. Here's why:

***Understanding "One" and "Three" in Different Respects**: The doctrine of the Trinity states that God is one in essence (or substance) and three in persons. A contradiction would occur if we were claiming that God is one and three in the same respect. However, the Church teaches that God is one in essence but three in persons. This distinction means there is no logical contradiction because the oneness and Threeness refer to different aspects of God's being.*

***The Unity of Essence**: God's essence is the single, indivisible divine nature that is fully possessed by the Father, the Son, and the Holy Spirit. This means that all three persons are equally God, sharing the same divine nature without division. The Church teaches that the divine nature is not divided among the persons but fully exists in each one.*

***The Distinction of Persons**: The Father, Son, and Holy Spirit are distinct persons, not separate beings. Their distinctions are not in what they are (as all are fully God), but in how they relate to each other. The Father is unbegotten, the Son is begotten of the Father, and the Holy Spirit proceeds from the Father and the Son. These relationships define their distinct personhood within the one divine essence.*

***Analogy and Mystery:** The Trinity is ultimately a mystery that transcends human understanding, meaning it cannot be fully* *comprehended by human reason alone. However, it is not irrational or contradictory. The Church uses analogies, such as the analogy of a triangle having three distinct angles but forming one shape, to help explain how three persons can exist within one God. These analogies are imperfect but useful for grasping the concept without implying contradiction.*

Philosophical and Theological Foundations*: The Catholic Church teaches that the mystery of the Trinity is a central tenet of the Christian faith, reflecting the depth and richness of God's nature beyond what human reason alone can fully explain.*

This is best explained in Philippians 2:6-9 "[6] Who, being in very nature God, did not consider equality with God something to be used to his own advantage; [7] rather, he made himself nothing by taking the very nature of a servant, being made in human likeness. [8] And being found in appearance as a man, he humbled himself by becoming obedient to death— even death on a cross!"[79]

PRIDE IS A SENSE OF SUPERIORITY, WHILE HUMILITY AND SELF-CONTROL ARE TWO PEAS IN A POD.

In Christianity, pride and humility represent contrasting attitudes and behaviors: Pride is often seen as an excessive focus on oneself, leading to arrogance, self-centeredness, and a sense of superiority over others. It involves an inflated sense of one's own importance and accomplishments, often accompanied by a disregard for others and their needs. In Christian teachings, pride is considered a sin as it can lead to rebellion against God and a lack of dependence on Him. Humility, on the other hand, is characterized by a modest and selfless attitude. It involves recognizing one's own limitations, weaknesses, and dependency on God. Humble individuals are willing to serve others, acknowledge their faults, and prioritize the well-being of others above themselves. In Christianity, humility is praised as a virtue exemplified by Jesus Christ, who humbled Himself even to the point of death on the cross, serving as a model for believers to follow.

Just as Martial arts often teach not to fight as a primary principle because their philosophies emphasize self-discipline, respect, and non-violence. While martial arts train individuals in combat techniques, they also promote using these skills as a last resort for self-defense or the protection of others rather than for aggression or conflict. Additionally, martial arts focus on developing mental strength and control, teaching practitioners to remain calm and avoid unnecessary confrontations through strategies such as de-escalation and conflict resolution. Ultimately, the goal is to cultivate harmony and peace, both within oneself and in interactions with others.

Jesus' humility on earth comes in the form of not taking advantage of the pleasures and luxuries He had in heaven as the Son of Man. Instead, He took it upon Himself to be among the sinners and the poverty that His people endured. He even suffered an agonizing death to save us from our sins. The example and teaching of His life on earth are in sheer contrast with those of the world. The world views humility as a weakness. The Christian concept of humility can be explained as a virtue that involves recognizing one's own limitations, faults, and weaknesses while also acknowledging the worth and dignity of others. It entails a modest attitude, prioritizing others before oneself, and being open to learning and growth. Humility in Christianity is often exemplified through the teachings and actions of Jesus Christ, who demonstrated servanthood and selflessness.

It is plain to see that it is only at the foot of the cross that Evil, Justice, Love, & Forgiveness converge at a single point in history. The death of Christ on the cross represents a confluence of the display of evil in men's hearts, but simultaneously, we see justice shown on the cross of Christ through the concept of atonement. The crucifixion of Jesus is seen as an act of divine justice where Jesus, who is considered sinless, willingly sacrifices Himself to pay the penalty for humanity's sins. This act demonstrates God's justice by providing a means for reconciliation between humanity and God, satisfying the demands of justice while also expressing divine mercy and love. The cross of Christ symbolizes the ultimate sacrifice and redemption, offering forgiveness and salvation to all who believe. His love was demonstrated in the final moments of His earthly life, as He uttered the words that pulsate in our hearts even to this day, "Father, forgive them, for they know not what they do." No wonder we cannot help but continue to preach Christ crucified unto Jews, a stumbling block, and unto Greeks' foolishness. [80]

Chapter 15

A Biblical Narration of Truth and Why This Journey Is
More Important Than the Destination?

Wrestling with Truth! In secular leadership positions, one
must refrain from placing their own self-interests before the actual
pursuit of the truth.

In settling workplace disputes, we are often in search of who
is right and who is wrong. In other words, we want to know the truth.
Similarly, in our daily discussions about the historicity of Jesus, we
are often confronted with the fundamental question: What is truth?

We all struggle with the definition of truth. The dictionary meaning typically states that Truth is the correspondence between a statement or belief and objective reality. It's what accurately reflects the way things are, devoid of personal biases or subjective interpretations. Our society, which includes every individual, irrespective of ethnicity or social standing, relies on the legal system to uncover the truth by evaluating evidence presented during legal proceedings. While evidence plays a crucial role in this process, the ultimate goal is to seek justice and determine the truth based on the available evidence and applicable laws. However, limitations such as the adversarial nature of trials and the potential for human error can sometimes affect the pursuit of truth within the legal system. If the existing flaws and biases in legal systems across the globe are a reality due to wrongful convictions leading to the incarceration of innocent individuals, their exact extent remains uncertain. Various initiatives aim to prevent and rectify wrongful convictions to address the issue.

If you read Matthew chapter 27, Mark 15, Luke 22–23, and John 18-19, you will find many details. They all contribute to the scene that happened regarding Pilate and Jesus. Here is the broader picture: Pilate could find no fault in Jesus and knew he was turned over to him to be sentenced because of envy of the religious leaders. Even Pilate's wife sent him this message to Pilate: "Do not have anything to do with that innocent man, for I have suffered a great deal today in a dream because of him."

Pilate then sent Jesus to Herod, but Herod sent him back to Pilate. Pilate told the crowd that neither he nor Herod could find any basis for their charges against Jesus. Pilate said: "Why? What crime has this man committed? As you can see, he has done nothing to deserve death. Therefore, I will punish him and release him." Pilate tried three times to convince the crowd to allow him to release Jesus. But with loud shouts, the crowd, led by the chief priests and elders, insistently demanded, "Crucify him! Crucify him!" Pilate answered, "You take him and crucify him. I find no fault in him." The Jews replied, "We have a law, and according to that law, he must die because he claims to be the Son of God." When Pilate heard this, he became even more afraid.

Pilate ordered Jesus to be beaten and flogged, then brought him out for the crowd to see. The soldiers had put a crown of thorns on him and a purple robe, mocking Jesus as being the king of the Jews. Pilate again appealed to the crowd. But the shouts prevailed even louder: "Crucify him! Crucify him!"

In the gospel narrative, a very interesting dialogue takes place between Pontius Pilate, the Roman governor of Judea (26–37 CE), who presided over the trial and then handed over Jesus to be crucified even though he found no fault in him.

In Jn 18:38…

"^{37} 'Then You are a king?' Pilate said. 'You say that I am a king,' Jesus answered. 'For this reason, I was born and have come into the world to testify to the truth. Everyone who belongs to the truth listens to My voice.' ^{38} 'What is truth?' Pilate asked and walked away. If only Pilate had waited for a response, he would have heard Jesus repeat the words that he spoke to Thomas in the 14th chapter of the gospel of John.

^{14} 'Let not your heart be troubled: ye believe in God, believe also in me.'

^{2} In My Father's house are many mansions: if it were not so, I would have told you. I am going to prepare a place for you.

^{3} And if I go and prepare a place for you, I will come again and receive you unto Myself; that where I am, there ye may be also.

^{4} And whither I go ye know, and the way ye know.

^{5} Thomas saith unto him, 'Lord, we know not whither thou goest; and how can we know the way?'

*^{6} **Jesus saith unto him, 'I am the way, the truth, and the life:** no man cometh unto the Father but by me.'*

^{7} 'If ye had known me, ye should have known my Father also: and from henceforth ye know him, and have seen him.'

^{8} *Philip saith unto him, 'Lord, show us the Father, and it sufficeth us.'*

^{9} *Jesus saith unto him, 'Have I been so long with you, and yet hast thou not known me, Philip? He that hath seen me hath seen the Father; and how sayest thou then, Show us the Father?'*

^{10} *'Believest thou not that I am in the Father, and the Father in me? The words that I speak unto you I speak not of myself: but the Father that dwelleth in me, he doeth the works.'*

^{11} *'Believe me that I am in the Father, and the Father in me: or else believe me for the very works' sake.'*

^{12} *'Verily, verily, I say unto you, He that believeth on me, the works that I do shall he do also; and greater works than these shall he do; because I go unto my Father.'"*[81]

In their frenzy, the mob accused, convicted and condemned the man, Jesus, because, from their limited perspective, they failed to recognize the truth of His divinity—not because of the absence of evidential truth, but because they placed their own self-interests before the actual pursuit of the truth. The claims that Jesus made were incomprehensible to the human mind in His day, and unfortunately, this remains the case even today.

Most of my life is spent managing and dealing with a myriad of problems and concerns. Life is also punctuated with joyful and fun times, which are both satisfying and fulfilling. However, if you stopped to plot a graph, it would most likely indicate that most of life is pain management punctuated by some occasional successes along the way.

In the book of Matthew 4:1-11 (New International Version), we are told that Jesus is tested in the wilderness.

¹ Then Jesus was led by the Spirit into the wilderness to be tempted[a] by the devil. ² After fasting forty days and forty nights, He was hungry. ³ The tempter came to Him and said, "If you are the Son of God, tell these stones to become bread."

⁴ Jesus answered, "It is written: 'Man shall not live on bread alone, but on every word that comes from the mouth of God."

⁵ Then the devil took Him to the holy city and had Him stand on the highest point of the temple. ⁶ "If you are the Son of God," he said, "throw yourself down. For it is written: 'He will command His angels concerning you, and they will lift You up in their hands so that You will not strike Your foot against a stone."

⁷ Jesus answered him, "It is also written: 'Do not put the Lord your God to the test.'"

⁸ Again, the devil took Him to a very high mountain and showed Him all the kingdoms of the world and their splendor. ⁹ "All this I will give you," he said, "if you will bow down and worship me."

¹⁰ Jesus said to him, "Away from me, Satan! For it is written: 'Worship the Lord your God and serve him only.'"

¹¹ Then the devil left Him, and angels came and attended Him."⁸²

How did Jesus respond to his challenges? In the above passage, you will notice that each time Jesus responded to the temptation, he was quoting scripture. All of Jesus' responses to those temptations came from the 6th and the 8th chapters of a very important book in the Old Testament. It is the 5th book of the OT, called Deuteronomy, which covers the history of the Israelites and their journey from slavery to the Promised Land. This book is often referred to as the most favored book of Jesus because he quoted from it frequently.

The Appointment and Limitations of Leaders.

Jesus reiterates this important truth for leaders and those in authority in the canonical gospels, where Pilate's court refers to the trial of Jesus in the praetorium before Pontius Pilate, preceded by the Sanhedrin Trial. "Do you refuse to speak to me?" Pilate said. "Don't you realize I have power either to free you or to crucify you?" Jesus answered, "You would have no power over me if it were not

185

given to you from above. Therefore, the one who handed me over to you is guilty of a greater sin."[83]

In the very first chapter of Deuteronomy, when Moses was chosen to provide direction and guidance as he was entrusted with the mammoth task of leading his people out of bondage and into the Promised Land. He quickly realized that he needed help and was humble enough to ask for it. He specifically instructed them that as leaders, they ought to be detail-oriented, unbiased, and courageous and to realize that they were simply the instruments of God. So, Moses spoke to his people **in verse** [9]*: "At that time I said to you, "You are too heavy a burden for me to carry alone.* [10] *The* LORD *your God has increased your numbers so that today you are as numerous as the stars in the sky.* [11] *May the* LORD*, the God of your ancestors, increase you a thousand times and bless you as He has promised!* [12] *But how can I bear your problems and your burdens and your disputes all by myself?* [13] *Choose some wise, understanding, and respected men from each of your tribes, and I will set them over you."*

[14] *You answered me, "What you propose to do is good."*

[15] *So I took the leading men of your tribes, wise and respected men, and appointed them to have authority over you—as commanders of thousands, of hundreds, of fifties, and of tens and as tribal officials.* [16] *And I charged your judges at that time, "Hear the*

disputes between your people and judge fairly, whether the case is between two Israelites or between an Israelite and a foreigner residing among you. [17] Do not show partiality in judging; hear both small and great alike. Do not be afraid of anyone, for judgment belongs to God. Bring me any case too hard for you, and I will hear it." [18] And at that time, I told you everything you were to do."[84]

1. Salvation was provided to the people with Moses in EXODUS (the Jews refreshed their minds during the feast of the Passover.)

2. Identity was defined on the mount SINAI (which was remembered at the feast of the Pentecost.)

3. They guaranteed preservation and were given a path to follow during their 40-year wandering through the wilderness (This was celebrated at the feast of the Tabernacles.)

So here we have a community that was redeemed, commanded, and blessed, yet things went wrong. WHY? It was because of wrong leadership. Leadership is critical in academia, in politics, in church and the home."[85] At the center of every establishment, there stands a man or a woman who must blaze the trail.

The history of Israel and its failure at the top was due to three main reasons, as we have already read in earlier chapters of this book:

*a) **The untamed and unbridled ego of a chosen person**
(SOLOMON)*

*b) **The licentious power of a privileged person**: (Solomon's
son REHOBOAM)*

*c) **The unteachable spirit of a person in need of self-
discipline** (JEROBOAM)*

*With the privilege of leadership comes the responsibility to
lead wisely. As Solomon's reign came to an end, Israel was divided
into two kingdoms. Why? Because of a lack of leadership
demonstrated on the throne. They failed to respond to the proverb
Proverbs 4:7, which states: "The beginning of wisdom is this: Get
wisdom, and whatever you get, get insight."[86]*

*How do you understand? You will undoubtedly agree that,
in hindsight, many of our disagreements and fallouts with people
are because of misunderstandings on both sides. Thus, it is logical
and prudent to recognize that by simply placing ourselves in other
people's shoes and seeing things from their viewpoint, we can, in
many situations, avoid such conflict. The epitome of this truth is
found in the person of JESUS, who placed Himself in the situation
of our place, even when he was himself sinless, only because He
knew that restoring our relationship with God was more important
than it was to prove that He was not at fault. In the Gospel of John,
we read, "But if anyone has the world's goods and sees his brother*

in need, yet closes his heart against him, how does God's love abide in him?"[87]

Lesson repeated: As I mentioned earlier, sometimes, if not most of the time, it is more important to lose an argument and win a relationship than it is to win an argument and lose a relationship. Once the relationship is not under threat of strain, you can always find a way to resolve disagreements with love and kindness at an appropriate time.

Colossians 3:12 ESV

"Put on, then, as God's chosen ones, holy and beloved, compassionate hearts, kindness, humility, meekness, and patience."

There is a Seasonal joke that goes like this:

Question: Why did the Israelites spend 40 years wandering in the desert?

Answer: **Because Moses refused to ask for directions**.

However, in reality, we see Moses often consulting with the Lord when he needed direction. We also see Moses, who, after all the miracles he saw and witnessed, asked God (Ex 33:14-16), "How will I know that you want me to get where I am going? God responded: "When you get there, then you will know."" God was teaching him a very important lesson and that a leader must realize that **the destination is not more important than the journey.**

It is no wonder that the windshield in our car is much larger than the rearview mirror. It is because where we are heading is more important than where we have been. Hence, we need to keep our eyes on the process of moving ahead rather than asking the question that little children often ask: "Are we there yet?" The journey itself has many of life's lessons we can and must learn from.

All the same, you are probably asking yourself a question: How do I get to the place God has chosen for me? The answer remains the same: When you get there, you can be certain that if it were not for GOD, you would have never made it. You see, God was leading the Israelites to the promised land, which should not have taken more than just a few weeks, but it ended up becoming 40 years of wandering in the wilderness. Yet you may insist on asking, "Why it takes so long... 40 years??" God answers this in Deuteronomy chapter 8: "To humble you and to test you to know your own heart and to find out whether or not you will keep my commands."

LESSON: The shortest route is not always the best route because it can bypass some of life's most important lessons.

Chapter 16

Humility

I recently watched a movie starring Denzel Washington. In the film, he is injured while trying to defend the defenseless. The doctor who was attending to his wounds asked, "Are you a good man?" The actor responded by saying, "I don't know". The doctor replied, "Only a good man would say what you just said." This story is similar to the one in which two priests were strolling in the garden surrounding their church. The younger priest broke the silence by asking the older priest. He asked, " Why do you think I sometimes question my own faith? Is it because I lack faith"? The older priest responded, "Only a truly humble and faithful priest questions his

own faith." What we learn from these two stories is that questioning our own abilities is crucial for personal growth and development. It allows us to identify areas where we can improve, challenge our limitations, and strive for excellence. By questioning our abilities, we open ourselves to new possibilities, insights, and opportunities for learning. This questioning helps prevent complacency and encourages a mindset of continuous improvement. Furthermore, questioning our abilities fosters humility, empathy, and a deeper understanding of ourselves and others. Overall, it promotes self-awareness and resilience, enabling us to navigate challenges more effectively and pursue our goals with greater confidence.

Yes, humility promotes self-awareness through looking inwards, through introspection. Introspection is the process of examining and reflecting on one's own thoughts, feelings, and experiences. It involves turning inward to gain insights into one's motivations, beliefs, values, and behaviors. Introspection can be done through various methods, such as meditation, journaling, or simply taking time to contemplate. This process helps individuals better understand themselves, identify patterns or biases in their thinking, and make more informed decisions. Introspection is a valuable tool for personal growth, self-awareness, and emotional intelligence.

Consider the story of András Toma, a Hungarian prisoner who was released from a Russian prison after 45 years. András

Toma (5 December 1925 – 30 March 2004) was a Hungarian soldier taken prisoner by the Red Army in 1944 and later discovered living in a Russian psychiatric hospital in 2000. He was probably the last prisoner of war to be repatriated. Because Toma had never learned Russian and no one at the hospital spoke Hungarian, he apparently did not have a single conversation in over 50 years—a situation of great interest for the fields of psychiatry. Initially, they thought he was mentally unstable until someone realized that he was simply speaking in an ancient Hungarian dialect. The story goes on to say that in all those approximately 56 years in prison, András had not looked at himself in a mirror. So, when he was released, the first thing he requested was a mirror, and when he saw his reflection and how different he looked now, he wept.

Humility is something like that. It allows us to put aside our pride and ego in order to take a closer look at ourselves from within. Hence, at a deeper level, the real question to ask is, "DO WE HAVE A MIRROR FOR THE SOUL?" God guides us through life in order to show us what we are really like. Only God can humble us without humiliation and exalt us and without flattering us.

King David was humble, but Saul was arrogant.

Philippians chapter 2:6-11 tells us to follow the example of Jesus: " Who, being in very nature GOD, did not consider equality with God, something to be used to His own advantage.

Rather, He emptied Himself and took on the nature of a servant, being made in human likeness and being found in the appearance of man. He humbled Himself by becoming obedient to death—even death on a cross.

Therefore, God exalted Him to the highest place and gave Him the name that is above all names, that at the name of JESUS, every knee shall bow, and every tongue confess that JC is Lord, to the glory of God the Father."

In a nutshell, Rev. Tony Cupit (Baptist World Alliance) beautifully **summarizes the qualities of an effective leader as he imitates the true leader, Jesus of Nazareth, who did not hesitate to wash the feet of His disciples. Jesus demonstrates that a good leader must also be ready to serve.**

"Effective leaders will be humble before God and before others. They will be humble, not servile, self-possessed, not selfish. They will not need to be applauded or praised. They will recognize that abilities owned will be the gift of a gracious God and will not have come through human achievement or natural talents. Therefore, they will not need to promote themselves, to boast, to posture to advertise their skills. Their humility will make them personally secure, not continually needing the affirmation of others".

One cannot create these unique and servile leadership qualities in a laboratory or even by simply reading a book such as this. It emerges from a strong willingness to be subservient to God. The Bible says, "Therefore I want you to understand that no one speaking by the Spirit of God ever says, 'Jesus be cursed!' and no one can say 'Jesus is Lord' except by the Holy Spirit."[88] It is only through the promptings of the Holy Spirit that we can develop a relationship with Jesus, our Lord and teacher.

Humility allows us to be open and receptive to new ideas and discover the potential that propels us forward. In doing so, we release attributes within us, such as Godliness, ethical and moral choices, the ability to build your home on a rock, to listen without judging, kindness and gentleness, perception and vision, and finally, common sense. I have discussed most of the attributes mentioned above. However, there is one attribute that we, as ethnological homo sapiens, often fail to draw upon: God-given common sense.

Common-sense

Perhaps this is the sensitivity of our conscience, which is imbued naturally. There are no scientific deductions or a particular formula. I am of the opinion that this is indeed the wisdom that God gave to Solomon. However, this wisdom is accessible to all who submit to the inner workings of the Holy Spirit. It can also be described as the theonomous inspiration made sensitive by God's laws to distinguish right from wrong, written on our hearts. This ability allows us to think on our feet by bypassing analytical deductions that often confuse us in times of crisis. The Scriptures tell us that all wisdom comes from above and those who are natural leaders, who have the gift of common sense, realize that this precious gift has indeed come from above.

Finally, in all human endeavors, we must recognize that the key to living a meaningful life is in one single word: "SURRENDER." In the gospel of John 15:5, Jesus says, "I am the vine, you are the branches. He who abides in Me, and I in him, bears much fruit; for without Me, you can do nothing." The Bible teaches us that only by dwelling in Christ and His love can we attain eternal significance and reap eternal rewards. Without Christ, we can do nothing of significance in the workplace which will continue to be followed by the people you led, even in your absence! We need to place our strengths, inability, and weaknesses in the WORD that became flesh. There is nothing to lose and everything to gain. Nothing explains this better than a poem, which I have repeated several times over and over again to remind myself of how much I need to rely on God for guidance.

The Rosebud [89]

by Pastor Darryl L. Brown

It is only a tiny rosebud

A flower of God's design.

But I cannot unfold the petals

With these clumsy hands of mine

The secret of unfolding flowers

Is not known to such as I

The flower God opens so gently

In my hands would fade and die

If I cannot unfold a rosebud,

This flower of God's design,

How can I have wisdom

To unfold this life of mine?

So, I'll trust in Him for His leading

Each moment of every day,

And I'll look to Him for His guidance

Each step of the pilgrim way

For the pathway that lies before me

My heavenly Father knows

I'll trust Him to unfold the moments

Just as he unfolds the rose

Chapter 17

Witnessing Ought to Come Naturally by Acting Out the Principles of Your Moral Convictions Without Offending Others.

Witnessing involves attesting to the truth or vouching for a truth claim. When you read Jn 18:37-40, Pilate asks Jesus, "What is truth"? And then he walks away. However, if he had to stay and listen for a response, he would have heard what Jesus said to Thomas in Jn 14:5-7[90] :

⁵ Thomas said to him, "Lord, we don't know where you are going, so how can we know the way?"

⁶ Jesus answered, "I am the way and the truth and the life. No one comes to the Father except through me."

⁷ "If you really know me, you will know my Father as well. From now on, you do know him and have seen him."

It is never easy or comfortable to "witness Christ" because we live in a world where there are agnostics, atheists, as well as those of different other worldviews, and then there are Christians who are indifferent to the message of Christ.

I heard a story about a ten-year-old orphaned boy who accompanied his new foster parents to church for the very first time. At first, he was uncomfortable as he looked around at all the families sitting quietly in their pews, all dressed up. He then heard the man at the pulpit talk about how a gentleman from a city called Nazareth went about touching people and making them well again. He cured the lame, the cripple, and the blind. He talked about love and kindness. He even fed 5,000 hungry people with a schoolboy's lunch. He even brought the dead back to life… "Wow," he thought, "This man was a superhero." Then, after hearing about all these good deeds, he learned that the man was unjustly accused, arrested, convicted, and condemned by fabricated lies and evil men. They sentenced him to die… "What, without any remorse?" he wondered. His hands were now tightly clenched into fists as he quickly glanced around, glad to be among all these people. "Now, surely, they would *do something about it," he thought. He now couldn't wait for church to be over. He wondered what all these people would do. Next to him in a pew sat a giant of a man. He wondered how this man and all the others would react. They must certainly want to rush over to defend this innocent man and make things right.*

Alas, after the sermon was over, he was amazed that people didn't seem quite so affected by what they heard. They greeted each other and simply chatted about mundane things like bake sales, hockey scores, golf tee-offs, and the upcoming barn dance, which they seemed particularly excited about.

Just like this young lad, how can one describe the apathy and impassivity of those around us? Our ears have become finely tuned to the latest and the greatest. The span of 2000 years has distanced many from the reality of the sacrifice made on the cross in 33 AD. It has numbed and dulled our memories, just as many of us have no impactful recollection of the Holocaust, which happened in our century.

Plato once said, "Rhythm and harmony find their way into the inward places of the soul." But it was Andrew Fletcher who famously said, "Let me make the songs of a nation, and I care not who makes its laws."[91]

Science is highly valued for its emphasis on empirical data and verifiability, but it is through the arts that philosophical ideas make inroads into the imagination using the backdoor of the mind to make us feel what we think.

"The phrase, a picture speaks a thousand words, was coined at one time, but a thousand years of experiences can be crunched in one meaningful rhyme,"—writes the author of this book.

How can we become so indifferent to the passion of Christ on the cross? The poem below by **Geoffrey Studdert Kennedy** *(1883-1929) describes how Jesus would react if he somehow were to take a flight to England or North America today.*

"When Jesus came to Golgotha, they hanged Him on a tree,

They drove great nails through hands and feet, and made a Calvary;

They crowned Him with a crown of thorns, red were His wounds and deep,

For those were crude and cruel days, and human flesh was cheap.

When Jesus came to Birmingham, they simply passed Him by.

They would not hurt a hair of Him, they only let Him die;

For men had grown more tender, and they would not give Him pain,

They only just passed down the street, and left Him in the rain.

Still Jesus cried, "Forgive them, for they know not what they do,"

And still it rained the winter rain that drenched Him through and through;

The crowds went home and left the streets without a soul to see,

And Jesus crouched against a wall, and cried for Calvary. "[92]

Let's look at the next best thing that God created – NATURE itself. Perhaps there is much to learn from the universe that God spoke into existence. We see wonders of nature like Niagara Falls, hurricanes and typhoons, weeds and roses. Are they trying hard to do what they do so well? [93] *"We stand in awe before the great natural wonders of nature, like the Grand Canyon, Mount Everest, the Great Barrier Reef, or the mighty Niagara Falls, deafened by its roar. The southern parts of the USA experience several hurricanes, waiting helplessly for the onslaught, unable to prevent it. Author George E Vanderman writes about how these hurricanes and tornadoes dip down to earth so powerfully on a mindless, unpredictable path of destruction. The forces of nature can be widespread and devastating, affecting various aspects of the environment and human life. These disastrous forces can turn everyday objects into dangerous projectiles, causing further damage to buildings, vehicles, and infrastructure and posing a significant threat to human safety. We are powerless before the forces of nature. We can file our insurance claims and mourn our losses. How does nature generate all this power? Does it try so very hard, or does it just pretend to be powerful? We would be utterly repulsed if the dandelions in our backyard pretended to be roses. Isn't it quite phony to watch the people in movies who pretend to be what they are not?*

Nothing seems more repulsive to the non-Christian than to meet a Christian whose practice of their faith is Artificial..."

Nature does not pretend. It only does what comes naturally!

Can God do the same with us, men and women? Yes, but not without the Spirit of God. Just as He did with Peter, the bungling fisherman, who on the day of Pentecost, spoke with authority (ACTS 2:22-47).

Peter is described as a shifting compound of loyalty to Christ and treacherous self-interest. Peter, the blundering disciple, ran away when he was needed the most and even denied knowing Jesus. After the outpouring of the Holy Spirit at Pentecost, Peter underwent significant changes:

1. Boldness and Courage: Peter, who had previously denied Jesus three times out of fear, became bold and courageous. He publicly preached to large crowds, unafraid of the authorities.

2. Leadership: He emerged as a prominent leader among the apostles, guiding the early Christian community and making important decisions.

3. Clarity and Understanding: Peter's understanding of Jesus' teachings and the Scriptures became clearer. He was able to interpret and explain them effectively to others.

4. Miraculous Works: Empowered by the Holy Spirit, Peter performed miracles, such as healing the lame man at the temple gate (Acts 3:1-10).

5. Conviction and Authority: His preaching carried a deep conviction and authority that led to the conversion of thousands, as seen in his sermon on the day of Pentecost (Acts 2:14-41). Overall, the outpouring of the Holy Spirit transformed Peter from a hesitant follower into a powerful and confident leader of the early Church. Instead, they showed a keen interest in a beggar. "Then Peter said, Silver and gold have I none; but such as I have to give I thee: In the name of Jesus Christ of Nazareth rise up and walk."[94] The crippled beggar went home cured, walking, leaping, and praising God. (he couldn't help praising GOD) Praising came effortlessly to him.

A DEEPER ASSERTION OF YOUR FAITH IN ACTION

The monkey in us: Successful leaders ought to let go and let God.

A story is told of an animal trapper who wanted to capture monkeys so he could sell them to zoos. The monkeys, however, were very clever, and every trap he set failed. A young boy watched the man's pathetic efforts and laughed.

The man said, "If you can catch me a monkey, I'll give you $2." (That was a huge amount of money then.)

The boy went to his home and took a clay pot with a narrow neck. He placed a few nuts around the pot and filled it with more nuts. He then tied the pot to a tree and told the man, "We should have a monkey in a few hours. Let's wait in the village. The monkey will call us when he is ready."

Sure enough, a band of monkeys soon discovered the nuts and the pot. One monkey slipped his hand into the pot and grabbed a handful of nuts, but he couldn't pull his hand out of the narrow opening of the pot because his fist was clenched. The monkey panicked and started making loud noises. Other monkeys tried unsuccessfully to pull the pot off his hand.

The boy and the man heard the ruckus, and the boy fetched a sack. As they approached all the monkeys ran away except the one with its hand in the pot. The boy grabbed both the monkey and the pot. The man was amazed and asked about the secret of the boy's monkey trap. "Why was it so easy for the monkey to get his hand in but so hard to get it out?"

The boy laughed and explained, "The monkey could have easily got his hand back out and escaped, but he would have had to let go of the nuts in the pot, and he just wasn't willing to let go. They never are."

What lessons can be learned from this story? Do people sometimes trap themselves by holding onto things that they should let go of? Do you?

This story is often used to illustrate the power of greed. People get trapped by the trappings of success, wealth, and a limitless desire to acquire and hold onto material things — even when the things they hold do not give them what they want or need. But there are other dimensions to the story as well. Many people trap themselves by holding onto negative feelings — resentment, anger, and jealousy — which both lessen and limit their lives. Like the monkey who gains no pleasure or nourishment from the nuts he holds in his hand, we can derive nothing of value from such negative emotions. Many of us could improve our lives instantly by the simple act of letting go.

The monkey in our anecdote does not suspect that he is being held prisoner solely by his mind. He has found some nuts. Greed — an unreasonable and unreasoning desire — has taken hold. Though the jungle abounds with fruits and nuts and all kinds of foods, his conditioned reaction dictates that he must have these as well. His narrow mindset is the only thing that imprisons him, that prevents him from letting go from seeing the absurdity of his predicament as well as the obvious way out of it.

C.S Lewis writes in the last paragraph of "Mere Christianity. Do I ever need to keep learning this every day? But there must be a real giving up of the self. You must throw it away "blindly," so to speak. Christ will indeed give you a real personality, but you must not go to Him for the sake of that. As long as your own personality is what you are bothered about, you are not going to Him at all.

Seek first the Kingdom of God... If you are seeking Him because you want all these things, then you are not seeking him at all. The very first step is to try to forget about the self altogether. Your real, new self—which is Christ's and also yours, and yours just because it is His—will not come as long as you are looking for it. It will come when you are looking for Him. Does that sound strange? The same principle applies, you know, to more everyday matters. Even in social life, you will never make a good impression on other people until you stop thinking about what sort of impression you are making.

Even in literature and art, no man who bothers about originality will ever be original. Whereas if you simply try to tell the truth (without caring how often it has been told before), you will, nine times out of ten, become original without ever having noticed it. The principle runs through all life from top to bottom. Give up yourself, and you will find your real self. Lose your life, and you will save it. Submit to death, death of your ambitions and favorite wishes every day and death of your whole body in the end: submit with every fiber of your being, and you will find eternal life. Keep back nothing. Anything that you have not given away will ever be really yours. Nothing in you that has not died will ever be raised from the dead. Look for yourself, and you will find in the long run only hatred, loneliness, despair, rage, ruin, and decay. But look for Christ and you will find Him, and with Him everything else thrown in. "[95]*

Luke 3:1 tells that in the fifteenth year of the reign of Tiberius Caesar—when Pontius Pilate was governor of Judea, Herod was tetrarch of Galilee, his brother Philip tetrarch of Iturea and Traconitis, and Lysanias tetrarch of Abilene during the high-priesthood of Annas and Caiaphas, the word of god came to John son of Zechariah in the wilderness. Among such important people, GOD chose to come to John the Baptist.[96]

Have you ever wondered how God used Joseph, who was raised in the desert, in order to use him in a palace, and Moses, who was raised in a palace, in order to be used in a desert? The hound of heaven selects those instruments in order to do some of His choicest pieces of work, and He finds them in the most unlikely of places.

Have you ever wondered about the circumstances that brought each of you to the lord? When you have gotten close to each other, you will be amazed to learn how God changed their surroundings in the most dramatic ways:

We see several examples of changed lives in the various Biblical accounts. For instance, in the book of Joshua, we see Rahab, who went from a harlot to a heroine; Joshua, a stone cutter, to a leader of men; Gideon, a farmer transformed into a military Commander; Peter, a bungling fisherman into a Fisher of men, and Paul a persecutor of Christians to the Pillar of Christ and his church and so many others.

It is only when we seek to know HIM and submit to Him only then do we begin to experience that God, the divine potter, can melt us, mold us and fashion us into vessels of HIS choice. Each one is distinct and valuable in HIS eyes – not ours and not the image we want to project to others.

Chapter 18

A Message to Young People Preparing to Get Into The Workplace.

The general goal of young people who are preparing to get into the workplace today often revolves around gaining valuable experience, developing professional skills, and establishing a foundation for their future careers. Additionally, They often seek financial independence, personal growth opportunities, and the chance to make a positive impact in their chosen fields. However, there is nothing inherently wrong with pursuing wealth to provide the best for your family and yourself. However, if the one who is your role model is prone to unethical behavior and your future is *shaped and influenced by people around you. Then, this work ethic will, over time, seem normal and acceptable in your own mind. This is a dangerous path to tread, and a good example is the Enron Corporation.*

Enron Corporation was an American energy, commodities, and services company based in Houston, Texas. It was founded in 1985 it was initially involved in natural gas pipelines and trading. Over time, Enron expanded into various other sectors, including electricity, broadband services, and pulp and paper. However, it became infamous for its involvement in accounting fraud and corporate misconduct, which led to its bankruptcy in 2001. The leaders at Enron were driven by a combination of greed, ambition, and a desire for personal gain. They engaged in fraudulent activities to manipulate financial statements, deceive investors, and inflate stock prices. Which ultimately lead to one of the largest corporate scandals in history. Their unethical behavior prioritized short-term profits over the well-being of employees, shareholders, and the public, resulting in devastating consequences for many people.

Christian youth in the workplace can benefit from learning about integrity, compassion, humility, and the importance of serving others. They should focus on cultivating a strong work ethic, enhancing communication skills, and the ability to work well in teams while maintaining their faith principles. Additionally, understanding the importance of ethical decision-making and consistently treating everyone with respect and dignity is also crucial. Once you develop a strong sense of what is right and wrong, it will become invaluable to you when you face temptations to do the wrong thing.

TEMPTATION: While it may be nearly impossible to prevent a bird from landing on your head, surely, you can certainly stop this bird from building a nest in your hair. We sin in private and hope no one is watching, which brings up the age-old question: If a tree falls in the jungle with no one there to hear it, will it make a noise? No matter where you go in scripture, you will find that the question of the sovereignty of GOD and the responsibility of man emerges.

Jesus himself said to his disciples, in the gospel of Luke 17:1, "Temptations to sin are sure to come, but woe to the one through whom they come!"[97]

Luke 3:7-9 John said to the crowds coming out to be baptized by him, "You brood of vipers! Who warned you to flee from the coming wrath?" [8] Produce fruit in keeping with repentance. And do not begin to say to yourselves, 'We have Abraham as our father.' For I tell you that out of these stones, God can raise up children for Abraham. [9] The ax is already at the root of the trees, and every tree that does not produce good fruit will be cut down and thrown into the fire." When Jesus referred to some followers as a "brood of vipers," He was specifically addressing certain religious leaders, particularly the Pharisees and Sadducees, who were known for their hypocrisy and deceitful behavior. Jesus used this strong language to condemn their hypocrisy and warn the people about the dangers of following leaders who outwardly appeared righteous but inwardly were corrupt and misleading. This phrase emphasized the severity of their actions and highlighted the need for genuine repentance and transformation.

This transformation is not a skill to be learned because it does not come from the outside but rather emerges from the inside. In the gospel of Matthew chapter 15 and verse 19, we are reminded that "For out of the heart come evil thoughts, murder, adultery, sexual immorality, theft, false testimony, slander."

You may find yourself in a workplace where unethical behavior is the norm, but if you are convicted to please God, not man, then you have two choices: find a different workplace, following the advice of Corrie Ten Boom, who wrote a book called, 'The Hiding Place' where she said, "I've learned that we must hold everything loosely because when I grip it tightly, it hurts when the Father pries my fingers loose and takes it from me!"[98]

But an even better approach is to become the instrument of change you want to see in others. C.T. Stud said, "Some like to live near the sound of Church or the chapel bell, but I want to build a rescue mission within one yard of Hell."

Today's youth will be tomorrow's CEOs. If the general idea is to Lord, it over your subordinates, then that is not a good way to start. Ambition is not a bad thing, but ambition must be entwined with critical thinking. I have had the opportunity to discuss various worldviews with young people around the kitchen table, where it became apparent to me that the general consensus is that the primary purpose of any religion is to make bad people good. This is quite true on one level, but on a deeper level, Christianity does not expect you to merit your salvation, like other major worldviews do, such as Judaism or Islam. Jesus says in the gospel of John 14:6, "**I am the way, the truth, and the life**: no man cometh unto the Father but by me."[99] Doing the right thing or becoming a good person emerges not out of compulsion or a need to gain brownie points with God but rather out of love for the one who gave his life for you, even while you were sinning. Romans 5:8 reminds us that God demonstrates his own love for us in this: While we were still sinners, Christ died for us.

Lesson learned: It is better to trust God and use our abilities than to use God and trust in our abilities.

Good leadership qualities are not just for workplaces. Leadership at home is equally necessary and plays a crucial part in shaping a productive, loving, forgiving environment that helps one another within the family unit to also succeed daily. This is what we sometimes call family values. This is not as easy as the culture you *aim to build in your workplace. It is even more delicate and personal. Love for an unforgiving, deeply troubled, and hurtful child, brother, sister, and spouse can make you extremely vulnerable. It is important to encourage a good family value system early in the relationship. No one realizes the extent of vulnerability you feel until you are entrusted with someone who depends on you and for someone you love. For working parents with a newborn, this vulnerability can be shocking, especially when you must entrust your child to someone else or even to total strangers in the absence of a willing and able grandparent or trusted caregiver.*

Just as in a working environment, it is easy to observe that in most, if not all, situations, the problems that are really upsetting are very rarely about the actual work you do. However, it is very often about the people you work with or report to. This is also applicable to family members, where you have much more to lose. A disagreement between grown-up siblings or between spouses can also be a burden that you carry to work. Sometimes, it's just the little slights and daily agitations that need forgiveness, the occasional sharp word or angry accusation. But we harbor it, let it eat at us, and build up bitterness and resentment, which erodes our relationship. We try to forgive, but a few days later, it's right there again, preying on our consciousness. Big wounds sometimes take longer to heal. They will come back to our minds. We stew over them and keep bringing them up, subconsciously attempting to punish those responsible for the hurt we have suffered. There is no way to avoid it. But every time they do, we must first remind ourselves that we really did forgive, then recall how much God has forgiven us and ask Him to take the destructive, unforgiving thoughts out of our minds.

When we feel hurt, and our ego is bruised, especially by someone whom we have grown to admire and love, then there is a great tendency to cut away the relationship rather than simply discard the ego and pride. However, when we take the easy route or bypass the difficult path, we also lose out on some of life's most important lessons to be learned. Always remember that it's better to lose an argument and win a relationship than it is to win an argument and lose a relationship. An argument doesn't always involve spoken words, and it also can take the form of passive-aggressive behavior of unspoken words spelling out resentment or simply giving someone the cold shoulder.

Forgiveness does not require a litany of justification and endless reasoning. This amounts to taking back with one hand what you just offered with the other. Instead, a genuine warm hug and a simple apology go a long way to healing hurting relationships.

Forgiveness does not necessarily mean that we must suffer in silence. When the threat of strain has been removed, and the ego has been set aside, it is also important under gentler circumstances for open and honest communication. This opens up a good-spirited dialogue where both parties can share what they think and how each one feels about what the wrong has done to us and how our mates or family members can help us get over it.

When relationships are strained, and our pride is hurt, sometimes it seems as though our prayers are not being heard. This is because our Lord wants us first to be in the right relationship with Him and hence reminds us in the New Testament gospel of Matthew 5:23-24 23: "Therefore if thou bring thy gift to the altar, and there. Rememberest that thy brother hath ought against thee; [24] Leave there thy gift before the altar and go thy way; first. Be reconciled to thy brother, and then come and offer thy gift."

I remember a very convicting and deeply introspecting hymn of unknown origin that we sing in my Toronto prayer group:

> *"It's me, it's me, O Lord*
>
> *Standing in the need of change*
>
> *It's me, it's me, O Lord*
>
> *Standing in the need of change*
>
> *Not my brother, not my sister*
>
> *But it's me, O Lord, standing in the need of change*
>
> *Not my brother, not my sister*

But it's me, O Lord, standing in the need of change

Not the preacher, not the deacon

But it's me, O Lord, standing in the need of prayer

Not the preacher, not the deacon

But it's me, O Lord, standing in the need of prayer

Not my father, not my mother

But it is me, O Lord, standing in the need of change

Not my father, not my mother

But it is me, O Lord, standing in the need of change."

Sometimes, these hurtful situations are lessons and opportunities to look inward, do some introspection, and see if there is something within us that needs change. This might require an honest reappraisal of our personalities or habitual patterns that need changing. God tells us how much our sin grieves Him; that is what divine discipline is all about. We do not discipline each other, but we can discuss steps that will help us avoid these same pitfalls in the future.

The Ten Commandments were not to be seen as values that were nice to have. They were, in fact, permanent and unchangeable. "You shall have no other gods before Me" was the first of his ten great commandments (Ex. 20:3).[100] Our omnipotent, omniscient

God, who spoke this universe into existence and who lives outside of space and time, humbled himself and became man. If we place our pride before our loving God, then I am afraid our pride and ego become our idols. Idolatry is not just carved out graven images. Truth be told, anyone or anything that we hold dearer than God is idol worship.

"Among the prosperous and affluent, among us, which is often the case, with prosperity comes moral and spiritual degeneration. Secularism and materialism captured the hearts of the people, and sin ran rampant. The list reads like twentieth-century America: swearing, lying, killing, stealing, adultery, drunkenness, perversion, perjury, deceit, and oppression, to name but a few. But the thing that grieved the heart of God more than anything else was the sin of idolatry (Hos. 4:12, 13; 13:2). The golden calves set up by Jeroboam I about 150 years earlier had opened the floodgates to every evil expression of Canaanite idolatry, including drunkenness, religious prostitution, and human sacrifice."[101]

Chapter 19

A Good Leader Is a Good Leader Everywhere, Especially Within a Family Unit

In my opinion, one of the main causes of the breakdown in marriages is SELFISHNESS.

I heard of a funny incident when, at the end of a busy day, a man and his wife were sitting at home on the veranda in the quiet of twilight, broken only by the sounds of the gentle wind and the swash of the waves. They were enjoying a glass of wine together.

As the sun slowly set behind the mountains, she broke the soothing silence, saying, "I love you so much I don't know I could ever live without you."

The husband, a tad surprised, asks, "Is that you or the wine talking?"

She replies, "It's me ... talking to the wine."

Several decades ago, we had just immigrated to Canada. We had no immediate or distant relatives nearby, and my family was young. My sweet, lovely wife was barely in her mid-twenties, along with my one-year-old daughter and four-year-old son. We had managed to get us a decent townhouse and were doing our best we could to keep ourselves afloat. At the same time, we had made some friends and acquaintances, particularly very fond of one family. It was in the very early hours of the morning when our landline phone began to ring. As many immigrants might agree, a phone call at such an ungodly hour often brings worrisome thoughts about loved ones.

It was the desperate voice of a dear friend not very far from where we lived. They were blessed with children barely in their pre-teens. He blurted out the words: "Newton, my wife is gone." Initially, I thought she had been involved in a severe accident or something along those lines. It was only when he explained that she had walked out on him and their children that the truth sunk in. This left both of us feeling reflective, emotional, in shock or disbelief, and perhaps experiencing a range of feelings such as sadness, confusion, anger, or even numbness. We knew that this was a desperate call for help, and even though we had no solutions, we decided that it was important to be supportive and understanding during such a difficult time. So, we bundled up our sleeping children and drove to their home.

The very first thing we did was hold hands and pray, asking God for His wisdom and solace at a time like this. We continued to provide moral support to our distraught friend and his children. We helped him to keep his mind focused on the physical and emotional well-being of the children first while he dealt with his own emotions.

Fortunately, this separation did not last long because just a few weeks later, he received a call from his wife, who realized that what she did was wrong and wanted to return to him and their family.

Forgiving a cheating spouse is a deeply personal decision influenced by individual beliefs, values, and the dynamics of the relationship. In Christian teachings, forgiveness is often encouraged, yet it's crucial to remember that forgiveness doesn't necessarily mean condoning the behavior or staying in the same relationship. It's about letting go of resentment and moving toward healing, whether that involves reconciliation or not. Ultimately, forgiveness is a complex issue that varies for each person and situation. My friend forgave his spouse, and they remained together for several decades after this traumatic phase of their lives, hopefully until death do them part.

God deals with unfaithfulness in this very short book named HOSEA, nestled in the pages of the Old Testament. It tells the story of a husband and wife, Hosea and Gomer.

The Book of Hosea is one of the books that are a part of both the Hebrew Bible and the Christian Old Testament. It's named after its central figure, Hosea, who was a prophet in the northern kingdom of Israel during the 8th century BCE. The book primarily explores the relationship between God and Israel, metaphorically depicted as the relationship between a husband (God) and his unfaithful wife (Israel). Hosea's personal life serves as an allegory for God's relationship with Israel, emphasizing themes of love, faithfulness, forgiveness, and the consequences of disobedience. The book is divided into two main sections: chapters 1-3 focus on Hosea's marriage to an unfaithful woman named Gomer, while chapters 4-14 contain Hosea's prophecies and messages to the people of Israel, warning them of the impending judgment for their idolatry and unfaithfulness, yet also offering hope of restoration if they repent.

Overall, the Book of Hosea is a powerful portrayal of God's enduring love and mercy despite human waywardness.[102] Noel, a long-time dear friend of mine, once advised that a successful marriage is when each spouse gives more than they receive. Selfishness can be detrimental to marriages because it undermines the foundation of mutual respect, trust, and support that healthy relationships thrive on. When one or both partners prioritize their own needs and desires over the well-being of their partner and the relationship as a whole, it creates imbalance, resentment, and conflict. Selfish behavior can manifest in various ways, such as neglecting the needs of one's partner, prioritizing personal interests over shared goals, or making decisions without considering their impact on the relationship. Over time, unchecked selfishness can erode the emotional connection between partners, leading to dissatisfaction, unhappiness, and, ultimately, the breakdown of the marriage. Successful marriages require compromise, empathy, and a willingness to prioritize the collective needs of the partnership over individual desires. Whatever stage of frustration you may feel in marriage, remember that a good marriage is about two imperfect people promising to work together by accepting their differences.

More than this, when trouble brews in a marriage before you reach for the phone, make it a habit to first go to the throne of God. You may be at the crossroads of a very depressing marriage at this time in your life. You are probably telling yourself, "Enough is enough," and you could be right if you are doing everything possible on your own steam. As Jesus tells us in the gospel of Matthew in chapter 19 and verse 26, "With men this is impossible, but with God all things are possible."[103]

Lesson: One can imagine many friends of Hosea who may have stopped and asked him why a teacher and an upright man like him would still want to have anything to do with such an unfaithful wife like Gomer. One can then imagine Hosea responding thus: "I am glad you asked me this question because now I understand why a holy God like that can still love an adulterous nation such as ours?"

Richard L Strauss brilliantly poses a question we all may be guilty of: "How many times should a husband or wife forgive? Some contend, "If I keep forgiving, I simply affirm him in his pattern of sin." Or "If I keep forgiving, she'll think she can get away with anything she wants." Others claim, "If I keep forgiving, it's like putting my seal of approval on his behavior." Or "I can't take another hurt like that. If he does that one more time, I'm leaving." Those are human responses. Listen to the response of the Lord Jesus. You see, Peter once asked the Lord this same question: "Lord, how often shall my brother sin against me, and I forgive him? Up to seven times?" The Lord's answer was, "I do not say to you, up to seven times, but up to seventy times seven" (Matt. 18:21, 22). That is a great deal of forgiveness. In fact, Christ was simply saying in a captivating way that there is no end to forgiveness.[104]

However, forgiveness does not mean that we will pay for the other person's offenses. Rather, we will refuse to retaliate in any way to make the guilty person pay. We will absolve them of all guilt. God can use that forgiving love to melt hardened hearts and change callused lives more quickly than anything else in this whole wide world. That is the lesson of Hosea and Gomer: the lesson of forgiveness. God's love and forgiveness pervade Hosea's entire prophecy. Please do not misunderstand: God hates sin; it grieves His heart; He cannot condone it; His perfect righteousness and justice demand that He deal with it. But He still loves sinners; He diligently seeks them out and offers His loving forgiveness.

God's ancient people, Israel, kept going back to their sins. "What shall I do with you, O Ephraim? What shall I do with you, O Judah? For your loyalty is like a morning cloud, and like the dew which goes away early." (Hos. 6:4). But God never stopped loving them. "When Israel was a youth, I loved him, and out of Egypt I called My son." (Hos. 11:1). "I led them with cords of a man, with bonds of love." (Hos. 11:4). "How can I give you up, O Ephraim? How can I surrender you, O Israel?" (Hos. 11:8). And because He never stopped loving them, He never stopped pleading with them: "Return, O Israel, to the Lord your God, for you have stumbled because of your iniquity." (Hos. 14:1).

Ravi Zacharias explains this flawlessly when he asks a very pertinent question, "Have you made a commitment to God? Have you ever said something to Him in your own prayer life? Time and time again, I think back to those moments when I came to a crossroads and made some commitments to Him. And then, as you start to stagger and struggle a bit, it is so good to go back to those moments and remember what you said to Him when He was moving in your heart so deeply. I understand that without emotion, marriage can be drudgery; however, I also understand that without the will, it can be a mockery. If you have not committed your will to anything, then something else owns you. Other than that thing, you're feigning any commitment."

When God calls you and me to be committed to Him, He is calling for our will. Not only does He love us, but He also asks that we remember what it is we promised Him when we came to Him. Bring your will, then move to God's response. God says in the book of Hosea 5:8-15 NIV, "⁸ Sound the trumpet in Gibeah, the horn in Ramah. Raise the battle cry in Beth Aven[1]; lead on, Benjamin. ⁹ Ephraim will be laid waste on the day of reckoning. Among the tribes of Israel, I proclaim what is certain. ¹⁰ Judah's leaders are like those who move boundary stones. I will pour out my wrath on them like a flood of water. ¹¹ Ephraim is oppressed, trampled in judgment, intent on pursuing idols.[2] ¹² I am like a moth to Ephraim, like rot to the people of Judah. ¹³ When Ephraim saw his sickness, and Judah his sores, then Ephraim turned to Assyria and sent to the great king for help. But he is not able to cure you, not able to heal your sores. <u>14</u> *For I will be like a lion to Ephraim, like a great lion to Judah. I will tear them to pieces and go away; I will carry them off with no one to rescue them.*"¹⁰⁵

Plainly said, I will beat you as a moth. I will beat you as a lion. And I will remove My presence and depart from you. A moth weakens, a lion tears apart. Further, He declares, "If my weakening of you doesn't change you, if my dismemberment of you in some way doesn't change you, I will have to remove My presence and depart from you."

This is where I look at our current cultural crises in North America. Clearly, we won't turn to Him by just becoming weaker. We may not even turn to Him when we are in some way mangled. But what I think is happening in our cultural crises today is a loss of wisdom. It seems we no longer understand right from wrong. We have no moral point of reference as a basis upon which to make our decisions. We talk about saving trees, but we forget that we have long neglected the TREE OF THE KNOWLEDGE OF GOOD AND EVIL!

Pastor Joe Wright's Prayer

"Heavenly Father, we come before You today to ask Your forgiveness and to seek Your direction and guidance.

We know Your Word says, 'Woe to those who call evil good.' And that's exactly what we've done. We've lost our spiritual equilibrium.

We've inverted our values.

We confess that we've ridiculed the absolute Truth of Your Word in the name of moral pluralism.

We've worshiped other gods and called it 'multiculturalism.'

We've endorsed perversion and called it an 'alternative lifestyle.'

We've exploited the poor and called it a 'lottery.'

We've neglected the needy and called it 'self-preservation.'

We've rewarded laziness and called it 'welfare.'

Father, in the name of 'choice,' we have killed our unborn, and then in the name of 'right to life,' we've killed abortionists.

We've neglected to discipline our children and called it 'building esteem.'

We have abused power and called it 'political savvy.'

We have coveted our neighbor's possessions and called them 'taxes.'

We have polluted the air with profanity and pornography and called it 'freedom of expression.'

We've ridiculed the time-honored values of our forefathers and called it 'enlightenment.'

Search us, O God, know our hearts today, try us, and show us any wickedness in us. And then cleanse us from every sin and set us free.

Guide and bless these men and women who have been sent here by the people of Kansas and who have been ordained by You to govern this great state. Grant them Your wisdom to rule, and may their decisions direct us to the center of Your will.

I ask it in the name of Your Son, the Living Savior, Jesus Christ.

Amen. "[106]

Happiness is a choice, and you must choose it well. The following poem explains it best:

POEM: My Choice

"I want my breakfast served at eight

With ham and eggs upon the plate

A well-broiled steak I'll eat at one

And dine again when day is done.

I want an ultramodern home.

And in each room a telephone.

Soft carpets, too, upon the floors

And pretty drapes grace the doors.

A cozy place of lovely things,

Like easy chairs with inner springs,

And then, I'll get a nice T.V.

- Of course, I'm careful what I see.

I want my wardrobe, too, to be

Of neatest, finest quality,

With latest style in suit and vest

Why should not Christians have the best?

But then the Master I can hear

In no uncertain voice, so clear:

"I bid you come and follow Me,

The lowly Man of Galilee."

"Birds of the air have made their nest

And foxes in their holes find rest,

But I can offer you no bed.

No place have I to lay my head."

In shame I hung my head and cried,

How could I spurn the Crucified?

Could I forget the way He went,

The sleepless nights in prayer He spent.

For forty days without a bite,

Alone He fasted day and night.

Despised, rejected - on He went,

and did not stop till veil He rent!

A man of sorrows and of grief

No earthly friend to bring relief.

"Smitten of God," the prophet said

Mocked, beaten, bruised, His blood ran red.

If He be God, and died for me,

No sacrifice too great can be

For me; a mortal man, to make.

I'll do it all for Jesus' sake.

Yes, I will tread the path He trod,

No other way will please my God,

So, henceforth, this my choice shall be,

My choice for all eternity."[107]

My final words to all who have read this book are the same words I started with:

"Attitude is a choice. Happiness is a choice. Optimism is a choice. Kindness is a choice. Giving is a choice. Respect is a choice. Whatever choice you make makes you. Choose wisely." We hear the phrase "the sky's the limit," a common expression used to convey the idea that there are no limits or boundaries to what one can achieve. On the other hand, those who have faith in Christ might see Him as the ultimate source of guidance, strength, and purpose in their lives, suggesting that their limits are determined by their relationship with Christ.

It's a matter of perspective and belief.

The sky is not the limit. Christ is!

Reference Page

1. Purportedly said by Franklin D Roosevelt

2. Blog by Darryl Davis, dated June 9, 2023

3. Extracts posted on August 23, 2011, from the Seven Habits of Highly Effective People by Stephen R. Covey, publisher Simon & Schuster.

4. Roy T. Bennett, author of "The Light in the Heart," Kindle edition, Feb 25, 2016

5. Blog at quickbase.com Top 10 Reasons Why Leaders Fail author Dan Schawbel August 21, 2013

6. 1 Kings 12:10 NRSV

7. Read "What Life Means to Einstein" by George Sylvester Viereck. Published October 26, 1929 [PDF].

8. Indian - Leader October 2, 1869 - January 30, 1948, Gandhi, Christ & Christianity, by Pascal Alan Nazareth

9. *"The Strong Name," Publication Year 1941, Author James S Stewart, Publisher: Charles Scribner's Sons*

10. *Gospel of John 14:6 RSVC*

11. *Der Spiegel, October 17, 1988*

12. *Richard Dawkins, River Out of Eden, publisher Basic Books, 1995*

13. *Has science buried God? Report from the Dawkins/Lennox YouTube Socrates in the city, Aug 21, 2019*

14. *Author Wendy Northcutt Darwin Awards II: More True Stories of How Dumb Humans Have Met Their Maker Hardcover – 25 October 2001*

15. *Principia, Book III; cited in Newton's Philosophy of Nature: Selections from his writings, p. 42, ed. H.S. Thayer, Hafner Library of Classics, NY, 1953.*

16. *https://en.wikipedia.org/wiki/Scientific_law*

17. *C. S. Lewis, Miracles (New York: Simon and Schuster, 1996), 140.*

18. *The Feynman Lectures on Physics Vol I, p 4-1*

19. *Principia, Book III; cited in Newton's Philosophy of Nature: Selections from his writings, p. 42, ed. H.S. Thayer, Hafner Library of Classics, NY, 1953.*

20. *Formulated by the philosopher Bertrand Russell (1872–1970),*

21. *https://memorial.billygraham.org/in-his-own-words/*

22. *Roy T. Bennett, author of "The Light in the Heart," Kindle edition, Feb 25, 2016*

23. *Luke 23:34 RSV*

24. *Amy Rees Anderson – Author, Oct 13, 2023*

25. *D. H. Lawrence, James T. Boulton (2002). "The Letters of D. H. Lawrence," p.248, Cambridge University Press*

26. *Bible Matthew 7:9-11 King James Version (KJV)*

27. *Bible Jeremiah 29:13*

28. *book Leadership is an Art publisher Crown Currency, May 18, 2004*

29. *Bible quote Genesis NRSV*

30. *Quote by the author of this book, Newton Fernandez*

31. *https://www.myaccountingcourse.com/accounting-dictionary/profitability, Shaun Conrad, CPA*

32. *Wednesday, June 5, 2013*

Excerpt of Dr. Ravi Zacharias' speech— Religious Liberty Paul Tillich last updated Dec 8, 2022, by Roger E Olson

33. Quote by Steve Jobs, Forbes Newsletter article by Victor Lipman, Sep 25, 2018

34. Quote by "The function of leadership is to produce more leaders, not more followers." — Ralph Nader. Todd M. Smith, M.Jun 16, 2017

35. Public Management and Organizational Change Winter 2007

36. Bible quote New International Version

37. Bible quote NRSV

38. Counterfeit Gods, author Tim Keller, Penguin 2011-10-4

39. Bible Quote NRSV

40. Hugh Whelchel: Exec. Dir. of the Institute for Faith Work & Economics). YouTube message by St Ignatius Catholic community on five lessons from the parable of talents, Nov 05, 2020.

41. Warner Bros movie, Chariots of Fire, March 30, 1981

42. Bible Quote NRSV

43. Author Nancy Pearcey, Total Truth, Publisher Crossway, Feb 28, 2008

44. *Tim Butler, from St Ignatius Catholic community, Jesuit church of Baltimore parable of Talents Nov 5, 2020*

45. *New Testament Luke 6:27-28 NRSV*

46. *Reem Kassis, contributor, former consultant, writer and cookbook author of The Palestinian Table, publisher Phaidon, Oct 23,2017*

47. *Reem Kassis, contributor, former consultant, writer and cookbook author of The Palestinian Table, publisher Phaidon, Oct 23,2017*

48. *Bible Quote Luke 15:4*

49. *https://www.starbucks.com/about-us/company-information/mission-statement*

50. *Posted by Michael Wilson in quotes on WordPress.com, Aug 2014*

51. *Dan Coughlin, keynote speaker, management consultant and executive coach*

52. *Bible Matthew 7:3 RSV*

53. *Kathy Miles – independent contractor Instructional Design/L&D) in her LinkedIn article dated Feb 12, 2017*

54. Work Cited Bible Questions Answered |
GotQuestions.org, http://gotquestions.org. Accessed 2 February
2024.

55. Author of this book

56. Author Thomas à Kempis, The Dover edition, published
2003, Translated by Aloysius Croft and Harold Bolton

57. Bible quote John 8:1-11 KJV

58. Bible quote

59. Bible quote RSV

60. 1 Peace: Henry A. Kissinger on Germany, February
2014 by Mirco Reimer

61. Christy DeSantis Chief Marketing & Communications
Officer | Health Enthusiast with Inner Science Geek | Confidence
Catalyst & Coach

62. John Lennox, Professor of Mathematics at Oxford
University

63. New Revised Standard Version Updated Edition

64. River out of Eden: A Darwinian view of life, by Richard
Dawkins Publisher Basic Books, 1995

65. Professor John Lennox YouTube lecture

66. King James Version

67. Poem by Kathleen Wheeler

68. Bible quote RSV

69. book How to read Job, Author John H Walton, publisher IVP academic, Sep 25, 2015

70. https://en.wikipedia.org/wiki/Tacitus_on_Jesus

71. Gary Habermas & Michael Licona (The Case for the Resurrection of Jesus, p. 59), Publisher Gregel Publications, March 26, 2004

72. Quest of the historical Jesus of Nazareth, author Bart Ehrman, Jan 01, 2013, Publisher American Atheist Press.

73. Matt 22:36-37

74. Book The Cry of a Lonely Planet, Author George E Vandeman, Pacific Press Publishing Association, 1983

75. 1 Corinthians 1:28 RSVC

76. Book The Cry of a Lonely Planet, Author George E Vandeman, Pacific Press Publishing Association, 1983

77. Geoffrey Studdert Kennedy, Priest and Poet. 1883-1929. / Vicar's Blog / By Revd. Ian Tattum

78. 1 Cor 15:14 NIV

79. New International Version

80. 1 COR 1:23

81. John 14:6 KJV

82. Matthew 4:1-11 New International Version

83. John 19:11 NIV

84. Deuteronomy 1 NIV

85. RZIM ministries teaching by Ravi Zacharias

86. Proverbs 4:7 RSV

87. 1 John 3:17 RSV

88. 1 Corinthians 12:3 RSV

89. The Rosebud, by Darryl L Brown, 1985

90. Gospel of John RSV

91. originated in an ambiguous sentence in Donald J. Grout's A History of Western Music (1973, p. 8).

92. Book The Unutterable Beauty, Author Studdert Kennedy, Jan 01, 1936, Publisher Hodder & Stoughton

93. Book The Cry of a Lonely Planet, Author George E Vandeman, Pacific Press Publishing Association, 1983

94. Acts 3:6:

95. Mere Christianity author C.S Lewis, publisher HarperSanfrancisco, revised Feb 28, 2023

96. *Bible Gospel of Luke 3:1*

97. *Bible gospel of Luke 17:1*

98. *"The hiding place," author Corrie Ten Boom, Year published: 1920-01-01 Year: 1971 - Random House Publishing Group*

99. *KJV Jn14:6*

100. *Exodus 23*

101. *Richard L Strauss expresses the Love of God for his people so eloquently in his series: Living in Love, 1978, Publisher Tyndale House*

102. *Bible, Old Testament, Hosea*

103. *Bible Matthew 19:26 RSV*

104. *Richard L Strauss expresses the Love of God for his people so eloquently in his series: Living in Love:*

105. *NIV bible Hosea 5:8-14*

106. *Pastor Joe Wright's prayer at the opening session of the Kansas Senate in 1996*

107. *By William (Bill) Pearce McChesney*

Martyred in Congo on November 25, 1964, at age 28.